Shane Groth & John D. Schroeder

Dear Lord,
I Want to Do
Daily Devotions

DIMENSIONS
FOR LIVING

NASHVILLE

DEAR LORD, I WANT TO DO DAILY DEVOTIONS

Copyright © 2005 by Shane Groth and John D. Schroeder

This book is printed on acid-free paper.

Library of Congress Cataloging-in-Publication Data

Groth, Shane M.
　Dear Lord, I want to do daily devotions / Shane Groth and John D. Schroeder.
　　p. cm.
　ISBN 0-687-05476-1 (binding: adhesive perfect: alk. paper)
　1. Spiritual life—Christianity. 2. Devotional exercises. 3. Devotional literature. I. Schroeder, John D. II. Title.
　BV4501.3.G77 2005
　242'.2--dc22

　　　　　　　　　　　　　　　　　　　　　　　　　2005018982

05 06 07 08 09 10 11 12 13 14—10 9 8 7 6 5 4 3 2 1

MANUFACTURED IN THE UNITED STATES OF AMERICA

To Andrew & Michael,
men of faith

S.G.

To Bruce Finger,
my friend for over forty years

J.S.

* Yellow markers: Holy Spirit message to me about Kurt. July/Aug 2007
* Green markers → ideas for talk on Ministry
* Purple markers → other talks?

Contents

INTRODUCTION 9
DAILY PRAYERS 13

WEEK ONE: Why Spend Time with God?

INTRODUCTION 15

Day One: God Has Found You 16
Day Two: God Has Chosen You 18
Day Three: Discovering God's Blessings 20
Day Four: Getting to Know God Better 22
Day Five: God Wants to Be Your Best Friend 25
Day Six: God Travels with You 26
Day Seven: Someone to Talk To 28
How Are Things Going? 30

Talk 1 (Priorities)

WEEK TWO: Eliminate the Roadblocks – Obstacles Talk

INTRODUCTION 33

Day One: Feeling Overwhelmed? 34
Day Two: Priorities 36
Day Three: Not in the Mood? 38
Day Four: Procrastination 40
Day Five: Time Management 42
Day Six: Finding a Place for God 44
Day Seven: Distractions 47
How Are Things Going? 49

WEEK THREE: Listening to What God Is Saying
INTRODUCTION 51
Day One: Hearing or Listening? 51
Day Two: How God Speaks to Us 54
Day Three: Receptive Body Language 56
Day Four: Intuition 58
Day Five: Focused Listening 61
Day Six: When God Is Silent 63
Day Seven: When God Answers 65
How Are Things Going? 68

WEEK FOUR: Living Your Faith Through Action
INTRODUCTION 69
Day One: What You See 70
Day Two: What You Say 71
Day Three: What You Hear 73
Day Four: What You Think 75
Day Five: What You Dream 78
Day Six: What You Have 80
Day Seven: What You Do 82
How Are Things Going? 85

WEEK FIVE: Living Your Faith in the World
INTRODUCTION 86
Day One: At Home 86
Day Two: With Relatives 89
Day Three: In Your Neighborhood 91
Day Four: In the Community 93
Day Five: At Work 96
Day Six: At Church 98

[handwritten margin notes: "wk 8", "christian action"]

Day Seven: In the World 100
How Are Things Going? 103

WEEK SIX: Go with God
INTRODUCTION 104
Day One: Good Works 105
Day Two: The Place of Prayer 107
Day Three: Praise the Lord 109
Day Four: Expect the Unexpected 111
Day Five: Let God Be God 113
Day Six: Life Isn't Fair. God Is. 115
Day Seven: Go with God 118
How Are Things Going? 120

Introduction

The desire to draw closer to God is as old as life itself. From the beginning, people have longed to be in touch with their Creator. Over time they have participated in worship services, drawn on the power of prayer, meditated in the wilderness, studied the Bible, sung hymns of praise, read spiritual books, and sought to make God a priority by every possible means. We have always been, and continue to be, seekers of God.

But what, exactly, is a *devotion*? A devotion is nothing more than a time to be "devoted" to God, a time to be with God. The *Merriam-Webster Collegiate Dictionary* (11th edition) says that a *devotion* is "an act of prayer or private worship." We just as easily could have titled this book *Dear Lord, Help Me to Spend Time with You!*

Our previous books *Dear Lord, They Want Me to Give the Devotions!* and *Dear Lord, They Want Me to Give the Devotion Again* attempted to take the mystery out of devotions by seeing them as a way for us to connect with God, either alone or with a group. The popularity of devotions is a testament to the need people have to spend time with God. Quiet time. A time to pray. A time to reflect. A time to seek God's will. A time to feel God's presence.

Yet while the desire certainly is there, when it comes to the practice of regular daily devotions, desire alone often is not enough. Our good intentions frequently are just a *longing* for God, and nothing more; it's experiencing that daily *connection* with God that is so elusive. If this is true for you, you are not alone. Many sincere Christians fail to spend time with God on a regular basis. We all want to grow in faith, but it is easier said than done.

Dear Lord, I Want to Do Daily Devotions is designed for those who desire to spend daily time with God but who need direction and encouragement to get started. It is not a "regular" book of devotions, but rather a plan of attack to turn desire into reality. This book offers forty-two devotions in a weekly format, along with encouragement to overcome whatever is standing between you and a daily audience with God. Our goal and your goal are the same: to make devotions a daily habit.

If you have been waiting for a nudge to get started, this is it!

This book is designed as a six-week spiritual adventure that guides you closer to God on a daily basis. Since it usually takes a minimum of three weeks to form a habit, we encourage you to read one of the devotions each and every day. This will be the start of a good habit, and one that can change your life. In time, you will find that spending just fifteen minutes a day with God will feel like sitting down and having a conversation with a good friend. As time goes by, you will find that this is the best time of your day. You'll enjoy this experience, and you will look forward to your time with God each day.

The format for each daily devotion is simple and flexible, and it offers a variety of activities. Each day begins with a brief scripture reading. It is followed by a short devotional reflection. (These reflections will cover a variety of topics during the six weeks.) A brief prayer follows the reflection. Next, the "Focus for the Day" is a one-sentence affirmation that will help you put your faith into action. And finally, your devotional time concludes with a time of personal reflection guided by a number of statements or questions. That's the pattern for your devotional time for the next forty-two days and beyond.

The choice is yours as to when to have your devotional time. You might want to experiment with different times during the day. Many people like to have their devotional time in the morning, to set a tone for their day. Or you may prefer to have your devotional time at your desk at work, during lunch. Or perhaps evenings are the best time for you to spend quality time with God. The key is to start a habit of doing devotions at the same time every day.

One idea that might help is for you to consider this time a daily appointment with God. Consider it an important meeting. Mark it on your calendar. Circle it in red. Take it as seriously as God takes you. Give God at least fifteen minutes a day to change your life. Call it a commitment, or consider it an investment in your future, because it certainly is. God wants you to succeed in this and to have the relationship with God that you desire. You will succeed to the degree that you make this a priority in your life.

In addition to each daily focus for your devotions, we have provided a weekly focus as well. The weekly introductions are designed to offer you encouragement and to get you thinking about a new dimension of daily devotions. The devotions for each week build upon the weekly introduction and will help provide direction for your thinking and your actions.

Do you like to keep track of your progress? If so, you'll appreciate the weekly evaluation chart that follows the final devotion for each week. Using this chart is optional; if it will help you stay on track, then use it. Use it daily if you desire, or do a once-a-week evaluation. The chart simply provides an opportunity for you to look back at the past week, think about the time you've spent with God, evaluate your progress, reflect on any challenges you may have faced, and take another look at your relationship with God. Again, the whole point is to encourage you in the habit of intentionally spending time with God each day. Use this evaluation tool if it helps.

Prayer is another way we get close to God, and this book offers some sample prayers to keep you in touch with God throughout the day. Take note of the simple daily prayers that are offered following this introduction. Use them—or prayers of your own—as often as you wish. Prayer will strengthen your connection with God and will help you sustain a habit of daily devotions. Prayer is another reminder that God is always present in your life.

And finally, speaking of prayer, read the title of this book. This title can serve as your prayer to God for help in beginning daily devotions. It is through the power of God that daily devotions will become an important part of your life. Today can be for you the beginning of a stronger relationship with the Lord. May you be richly blessed as you begin this six-week journey!

Daily Prayers

The following simple prayers can be read silently or out loud, on your own or with a group. Choose a prayer that appeals to you, or create your own prayer. Prayers remind us that God is with us throughout the day.

PRAYERS IN THE MORNING

Thank you for your blessings, Lord.
Help me use the gifts and talents you've given me
to bless others throughout the day. Amen.

Good morning, Lord! Thank you for the gift of this new day. Help me see the opportunities before me to draw closer to you today, that I may learn more about your wonderful world. Amen.

PRAYERS BEFORE MEALS

Lord, thank you for this food and for your daily blessings. Amen.

For this food, dear Lord, we thank you, and for all the many blessings you have provided. Amen.

PRAYERS BEFORE BEDTIME

Thank you, Lord, for keeping me safe today.
All my worries and sorrows I lay before you;
Let me rest in your love and grace until the morning light. Amen.

Thanks for another day, O Lord. I give to you all the problems and concerns that have troubled me today, knowing that you will take care of them in your own time and in your own way. Amen.

WEEK ONE
Why Spend Time with God?

Introduction

You are faced each day with decisions about how you are going to spend your time. If you are reading this, you obviously have taken the first step in deciding that you want to spend more time with God. But *why* do you want to spend time with God?

Is it because you think it's the right thing to do? Is it because you feel guilty? Is it because you have nothing better to do? Let me dare to answer the question for you. You have decided to spend time with God because God is calling you to do so. God has named and claimed you at Creation and is now calling you to spend time in this unique relationship. You have heard God's call, and you have responded. Congratulations! You might not feel as though God has been a part of this decision, but that has been God's role from the day you were born: to prod, nurture, and love you. In short, to call you "home," to connect your heart with the heart of God.

Think of this time as simply a time of connecting; a time to sit and reflect—and even wander—in the presence of God. Take it easy. Relax! Don't pressure yourself to do this or that, and don't worry about results; let God take care of that. Simply delight in this time with God, and trust that God will use it for your good, now and into eternity.

Day One   **God Has Found You**

Toward evening they heard the LORD God walking about in the garden, so they hid themselves among the trees. The LORD God called to Adam, "Where are you?"

—Genesis 3:8-9 NLT

About this time you might be asking yourself, *How does this devotion thing work? How do I spend this time "devoted" to God? Where do I start?* Or your question could be more general, as general as life itself: *Why am I here? What am I supposed to do now?* You might even feel a bit awkward, as though you were struggling to make conversation with someone you just met, wondering, Now *what?*

We might be tempted to start this journey with God by starting the same way most of us would begin any other endeavor—focusing only on what *we* can do. We start with our own actions first. We begin by trying to find God. Like playing hide and seek, we go looking for God in the hidden places, trying to find where God is located. We go to church. We join a prayer group. We start a Bible study, trying to pinpoint exactly where God is. But we do not find God; God finds us. The Bible, in fact, from start to finish relates how God keeps finding and calling back God's people. It is God who does the seeking, and it is always God who does the finding.

While Adam and Eve had never heard of the word *devotion* before, they were practicing it from the time they were created. The way to start is to respond to God, not to search God out. God calls, we respond. You don't have to locate God. God is already here. God has found *you*. God has always found you and has always been with you. As with Adam and Eve, God is walking about in the places we live and frequent, God is with us in our own "gardens" and homes, wherever that might be. And God asks us the same question God asked Adam: "Where are you?"

That's a rather funny question for God to ask, don't you think? As a seminary professor asked during class one day, "Has the all-knowing, all-powerful, omnipresent God already lost the only two people he created just a short time before?" Of course not. God knows exactly where Adam and Eve are. God is merely looking for a response, a word from the person he has created for himself.

Funny thing, isn't it, that our response, like that of Adam and Eve, is often to hide from God, to keep a safe distance from God. Whether it's a busy schedule or work or just trying to make ends meet, we find ways to avoid God and to keep our distance. But God does not keep distance from us—God is already here. God has found you.

"Where are you?" God asks you today. "Where are you? I'm looking for you because I want to spend time with you."

You can simply respond, "I'm here, Lord. Right here."

PRAYER

Dear God, thank you for finding me and for your desire to spend time with me. You are always looking for me, looking for ways to call me back to you. Help me make myself available, Lord.

FOCUS FOR THE DAY

Today I will remember that from the start, God has always found me.

PERSONAL REFLECTION TIME

Think of times in the past when you felt a yearning for God, or when you felt that God had called to you or "found" you. How did you respond to God's calling to be with you? In what ways have you tried to "find" God in the past?

Day Two   **God Has Chosen You**

*So God created people in his own image; / God patterned them
after himself; / male and female he created them.*
                                                —Genesis 1:27 NLT

The elementary school kids gathered in a circle, some
with sweaty palms, others with quickened heartbeats, still
others with a growing sense of nausea. They came together
at the playground to carry out the daily ritual of judgment
and condemnation: choosing sides for kickball. It wasn't
too bad if you were a good player, or if you routinely were
one of the first chosen for a team. But more than a few
prayers were said by those children who were less talented
athletically or less popular among their peers, that they not
be the last one chosen. Even second-to-last was acceptable.
But being the last one chosen meant you were a loser, not
much better than a target for the other team to aim for.

If this sort of thing didn't happen at the school playground, then no doubt it happened among friends or in
games played at the neighborhood park—people choosing
those whom they wanted on their team. And the ritual continued into middle school and high school in sports, band,
choir, school plays, cheerleading, and school dances.
People made choices about whether they wanted you to be
on their side.

Not much has changed since we've become adults.
Choices are made daily at our jobs about who wants us to
be on their team because of our looks or our brains or our
skills or our friends. And when we go home to relax, we
often get bombarded with more of the same in the form of
"reality"-based television shows such as *Survivor,
American Idol, The Bachelor,* and *Elimidate,* which remind
us that when it comes to other people, if choices are
involved, we may or may not be the one who ends up in
the winner's circle.

Thankfully, things are different when it comes to God. God always wants you on his side, and God is the first one to choose you to be God's own. Not only did God choose you from the very start of Creation, but he created you himself, created you unlike anything else he had created before. God wanted so much for you to be like him that he created you in his image. And God made sure this was recorded at the beginning of his book, in the very first chapter of the Bible, in the story of Creation, so that you would know it from the very start: "So God created people in his own image; / God patterned them after himself; / male and female he created them" (Genesis 1:27 NLT).

It didn't happen this way with the plants. It didn't happen with the animals. It didn't happen with the birds or the great sea creatures or the yellow-spotted thingamajigs. It was only with human beings that God made sure we were created like him, so that we might have a relationship with him, a kindred spirit, a connection of some kind.

You have been chosen by God. You were picked *first*. You were not the last of the litter; rather, you were the best of the bunch. Not because of what you did, but because of what God did. God chose you and created you in his image so that God could spend a lifetime, then an eternity, with you. Now, *that* is a choosy God!

PRAYER

Dear God, thank you for choosing me from the very start, not because of what I have done, but because of what you have done for me. Thank you for creating me in your image and for giving me a spirit that longs to be with you. Amen.

FOCUS FOR THE DAY

Today I will remember that God has chosen me to have a relationship with him.

PERSONAL REFLECTION TIME

Think about the many ways you choose others to be part of your life on a daily basis. How did you choose your friends? When have you been hurt by the choices of others to leave you out of something? Is it hard for you to believe that God has chosen you as a special part of creation, so that you might spend time with God and have a relationship with him? Why or why not?

Day Three   **Discovering God's Blessings**

The blessing of the LORD *brings wealth, / and he adds no trouble to it.*

—Proverbs 10:22 NIV

The more time you spend with God, the more clearly you can see how God has blessed you. Spending time with God opens your eyes to all you have been given by the One who loves you.

Henry Ward Beecher explained it this way: "So many are God's kindnesses to us, that, as drops of water, they run together; and it is not until we are borne up by the multitude of them, as by streams in deep channels, that we recognize them as coming from him."

Yes, we are swept away by the blessings of God. To say it another way, we drown in God's goodness. And yet, how often do we fail to see the hand of God supplying all our daily needs? It's more than food, shelter, clothing, good health, a job, friends, and family. The kindness of God begins the day we are born, with the very special gift of life. We are blessed from the very beginning.

As we begin to spend more time with God, blessings come into focus. As with drops of water, we still can't count all the blessings, but we recognize the Source. Our eyes are opened to the hands of God in our life. "Amazing coincidences" and "bits of good luck" are no longer anonymous gifts. We are able to clearly see God the Giver of our blessings.

Think back on your closest friendships. They probably didn't happen overnight. It usually takes an investment of time, mutual activities, and plenty of conversation in order to gain the blessings of a close relationship. It's the same way with God. The better we know God, the more comfortable our relationship with God becomes. And that opens the door for opportunities beyond our imagination, courtesy of our Lord Jesus Christ!

The blessings of the Lord do bring wealth, but it's often in the form of things that money can't buy—things such as contentment, inner peace, and true joy. These are all products of a strong faith based on a growing relationship with God.

So as you invite God to be part of your day, thank God for all that you have been given. You are more than just lucky; you are blessed.

PRAYER

Dear God, thank you for providing more blessings than I can count. Open my eyes so that I can see how many aspects of my life you touch. You are a God who cares about the details and who desires the very best for all your children. Help me to hear your voice throughout the day, and to take the time each day to build a closer relationship with you. Amen.

FOCUS FOR THE DAY

Today I will count my blessings and strive to be a blessing to others.

Reflect on what it means to have a continuing relationship with God. How does this reality shape your future? What kind of relationship with you do you think God desires? Think about the many blessings—those past, present, and future—that come from spending time together with God. Consider how you can be a blessing to others by passing along the many blessings God has given you.

Day Four   **Getting to Know God Better**

But as for me, how good it is to be near God! / I have made the Sovereign LORD my shelter, / and I will tell everyone about the wonderful things you do.

—Psalm 73:28 NLT

One of the reasons we spend time with God is so that we might get to know God better. After all, how can we get to know someone if we never spend any time with that person? Perhaps you have had experiences in your own life where you had doubts about other people, but after spending some time talking with them and being around them, you grew to like them. Perhaps they even became your very good friends.

The more time we spend with people, the more we hear them talk, the more we really listen to what they are saying, the more information we have to see what they are really like and to see what we have in common with them. The same is true with getting to know God. The more we hear God talk (by reading Scripture), the more we listen to what God is saying (through Scripture, through prayer, and through other people), the more we get to understand how great and loving and forgiving this God of ours really is. And as we get to know God better, we are better able to admit to God our own shortcomings, and we can receive the help God is waiting to so willingly give us. With whom do you share your most intimate thoughts, your fears, and your mistakes? If anybody, most likely it is your best friend. We can bare our souls to those we are close to because we know they will accept us for who we are. But this process does not happen overnight; it takes time.

At first glance, you might think that the writer of Psalm 73 trusted God every day, every minute, with his whole life. This psalm was written by Asaph, who is attributed with having written twelve psalms (Psalms 50, 73–83). Asaph was part of the group of musicians who oversaw the worship music in the Temple for King David (see 1 Chronicles 6:39; 16:4-5), and he certainly spent a great deal of time with God, worshiping in the Temple. But even Asaph had doubts, and in Psalm 73 he expresses them almost from the beginning. Asaph wonders why God is letting evil people prosper. The people want to know, he says, "Is the Most High even aware of what is happening?" Asaph continues, "Look at these arrogant people— / enjoying a life of ease while their riches multiply" (Psalm 73:11-12 NLT).

The plea then becomes personal for Asaph:

Was it for nothing that I kept my heart pure
and kept myself from doing wrong?
All I get is trouble all day long;
every morning brings me pain. (verses 13-14 NLT)

But over time, Asaph makes a discovery.

Then one day I went into your sanctuary, O God,
and I thought about the destiny of the wicked.
Truly, you put them on a slippery path
and send them sliding over the cliff to destruction.
In an instant they are destroyed,
swept away by terrors. (verses 17-19 NLT)

We may reach a different conclusion than Asaph about whether God brings destruction, or whether those who do evil bring destruction upon themselves. But the point is, by spending time with God (note that it was in the sanctuary—the place where God was understood to reside at the time), Asaph discovered a truth about the world and about God that earlier had him dismayed and distressed: "My spirit may grow weak, / but God remains the strength of my heart; / he is mine forever" (Psalm 73:26 NLT).

And so it is true for us. While our opportunities for being in God's presence are not limited just to the sanctuary or the church, spending time with God helps us discover God's ways and how we fit into God's overall plan. And like Asaph, we can be moved from doubt to telling others about all of the wonderful things God is doing.

PRAYER

Dear God, thank you for giving me the opportunity to spend time with you. Help me come to know you better over the coming weeks, and open my heart to your truth. Amen.

FOCUS FOR THE DAY

Today I will remember that spending time with God helps me get to know God better.

PERSONAL REFLECTION TIME

Think of your best friend or a friend from the past. Did you like him or her immediately? How often did you spend time together? Did spending time with your friend help you get to know him or her better, and if so, in what ways?

Day Five   **God Wants to Be Your Best Friend**

For I am persuaded, that neither death, nor life, nor angels, nor principalities, nor powers, nor things present, nor things to come, Nor height, nor depth, nor any other creature, shall be able to separate us from the love of God, which is in Christ Jesus our Lord.
—Romans 8:38-39 KJV

The minister of a large Washington, D.C., church answered his telephone and was asked if he knew whether the President of the United States would be attending Sunday services there. "That's something I can't promise," replied the minister. "But I do know that God will be there, and that's the best incentive I know for being in church this Sunday."

It's an awesome thought: You regularly have the opportunity to be in the presence of God, the Creator of heaven and earth! God is available to you, any time, any place. And not only that; God wants a relationship with you. God wants to be your best friend! Can it get any better than that?

The familiar hymn "What a Friend We Have in Jesus" celebrates this wonderful relationship we have with our Lord. Jesus, God's own Son, is our faithful companion who desires to share our burdens. We can bring anything to our Lord in prayer. Our devotional time is a time to connect with this loving God and to build a friendship that lasts an eternity.

Getting to know God takes time. God already knows you; you need to spend time getting to know God. Through prayer, meditation, and devotions, your friendship with God will deepen. God will become more a part of your daily life and thoughts. Not only will you discover the meaning of friendship, but also your life will be transformed as you become more like Jesus.

As you spend time with God today, remember the friendship factor. Learn more about this friend who wants you to succeed in life and who has the answers to all of your

25

questions. Confide in God, and listen for God's voice. God is present now. Know that God is listening to you, and that God wants to be your best friend. It doesn't get any better than that!

PRAYER

Dear God, thank you for the gift of friendship. Help me grow in friendship with you and treasure our special relationship. Encourage me in my prayer life. Teach me how to be a real friend to others and to be your servant on this earth. Remind me that you are always present when I feel lost or alone. You are my best friend. Amen.

FOCUS FOR THE DAY

Today I will walk with my friend Jesus, who is the Savior, God's only Son, and I will seek to do God's will.

PERSONAL REFLECTION TIME

Reflect on what it means to be a friend and to have a friend. What qualities do you look for in a friend? How are you a friend to others? Think about how friendship with other Christians can help you in your friendship with God.

Day Six **God Travels with You**

Now the LORD said to Abram, "Go from your country and your kindred and your father's house to the land that I will show you." . . . So Abram went, as the LORD had told him; and Lot went with him. Abram was seventy-five years old when he departed from Haran.

—Genesis 12:1, 4 NRSV

Read Before
footprints

Journeys have a way of changing us. Not only do we learn about the places we visit, but we also have an opportunity to learn more about ourselves. Journeys take us out of our daily routine, away from the comforts of home, and they allow us to discover new places and new people.

You are on a spiritual journey with God. Some of the landscape may seem familiar, and some of it may seem unknown. But as you travel on this journey, not only are you going to learn more things about God, you also are going to learn more about yourself. And if you give God the chance, you will be changed. You will be changed into the person God wants you to be.

God said to Abram, "Go from your country and your kindred and your father's house to the land that I will show you" (Genesis 12:1). And without question or complaint, Abram left. *What? He left? Just like that? Without assurances or letters of introduction or a survival kit or a GPS?* If asked, could you pack up all of your belongings and leave your relatives and home behind, simply because God asked you to? In a sense, this *is* God's request to you—to leave behind the assumptions and preconceived thoughts and personal baggage you have about God and to start anew. Open your life to God with a clean slate, and see what wonderful things God has in store for you.

It is said that before Christopher Columbus set sail for the New World, the king of Spain had coins minted with the inscription *Ne Plus Ultra*, which means "There is nothing beyond." After Columbus discovered America, however, the king had the coins re-minted with the inscription *Plus Ultra*, meaning, "There is something beyond." In your journey, too, there will be something beyond what you already know about God. Any boundaries and limits you have placed on God will be tested. God will come to you in new and surprising ways if you are open to the working of the Holy Spirit. So set your sails, and give God room to work. Let the journey begin.

PRAYER

Thank you, God, for the opportunity to begin this journey. Thank you for being with me as I move forward to discover more about you. Keep my mind and heart open to the many ways in which you work. Amen.

FOCUS FOR THE DAY

Today I will not put any limits on the ways in which God can work in my life.

PERSONAL REFLECTION TIME

Think of a favorite trip, vacation, or journey you have taken in the past. In what ways did you learn about the place or person you visited? What did you learn about yourself? How was the experience different from what you had expected? In what ways have you limited God in the past? How might you be more open to the ways in which God can work in your life?

Day Seven   **Someone to Talk To**

The LORD is my shepherd, I shall not want.
*   He makes me lie down in green pastures;*
he leads me beside still waters;
*   he restores my soul.*

—Psalm 23:1-3 NRSV

Have you ever thought about how fortunate you are if you are able to sit down and have an honest conversation with someone? Some people don't have that luxury. There are many lonely people in the world who lack a sympathetic ear. Others can't be "real" with another person because they carry a burden or a secret they feel they can't share. There is often a fear of being judged or rejected that also prevents honest dialogue. Who do you go to when you need to talk?

One of the reasons we need to spend time with God is to have that honest conversation we all need. Hopefully, the Lord has provided you with a close friend or a family member with whom you can share your ups and downs. But a conversation with your Creator adds an entirely different dimension to life. God knows your thoughts, desires, and feelings. God created you and has been with you every second of your life. No one understands you better or loves you more.

When you talk with God, you learn about God. That's what happens in any conversation. You gain information. At times in your praying it may seem that you are doing all of the talking and that God is just listening, but as your relationship with God progresses, you will realize that God is communicating with you. It may come as a feeling. You may be led by the Holy Spirit to walk a new path. The Lord does work in mysterious ways, and having regular conversations with the Almighty is the beginning of a changed life.

God's timing certainly may be different from yours. That's the chance you take when you strike up a conversation with God. You may have an expectation of what will happen, and yet you may be surprised. What makes our conversations with God different from those we have with family and friends is that God sees the big picture and delivers what is best for us. You may not get what you want, but God always provides what you need.

As you spend time with God today, know that God cares. God cared so much that he sent us his only Son, Jesus, who died upon the cross. Have an honest conversation with this friend of yours. Use this time to connect with the Eternal. Share what is in your heart. You will find peace and rest for your soul as you continue to walk and talk with God.

PRAYER

Dear God, thank you for listening to me. Thank you for being there for me at all times. Help me remember that I can come to you with all of my problems. I can depend upon you to help me sort it all out. Not only are you a caring God, you also are my source for a real and productive life. Remind me of your presence as I continue my day. Amen.

FOCUS FOR THE DAY

Today I will have an honest conversation with God.

PERSONAL REFLECTION TIME

Reflect on what you want God to know. Examine your thoughts, feelings, desires, and actions. Be honest in your conversation. Ask for guidance in your life. Feel the presence of God throughout the remainder of the day.

How Are Things Going?
Week One

While God is not keeping score up in heaven in regard to your daily devotions and prayers, the following chart is provided as a way for you, if you are so inclined, to keep yourself accountable on a daily basis. If you absolutely detest filling in charts, you might be more comfortable checking in with a member of your family or with a friend to talk about your growth and the obstacles you are encountering as you develop your devotional life. The goal is to keep yourself accountable. Spending time with God does not happen by itself, especially at first. Like forming any habit, it takes time, consistency, and patience to make time for God a daily practice.

Filling in the Chart

DAILY DEVOTIONS

For each day of the week, first, record the date. Then, make a check mark in the box for each section of the daily devotion you complete, including Scripture, Devotion, Prayer, Focus for the Day, and Personal Reflection Time. (If you complete every section listed, you'll have five check marks for each daily devotion.) Don't worry about leaving blank spaces on the chart, but do try to get at least one check mark per day. If you happen to miss a day, simply fill in the date when you get to the next day's devotion.

This chart is not a test, where every blank must be filled in. Rather, it is a way to help you see that you are making progress in spending time with God on a daily basis, however that may happen. Lastly, give thanks for every check mark you see, and look forward to your next meeting with God.

DAILY PRAYERS

Use the Daily Prayers section of the chart to track your prayer consistency. The goal here isn't to have a check mark in every box, but to develop intentional times throughout the day when you spend time talking with God in prayer.

		Sun	Mon	Tues	Wed	Thurs	Fri	Sat
Daily Devotion	Date							
	Scripture							
	Devotion							
	Prayer							
	Focus for the Day							
	Reflection Time							
Daily Prayers	Morning							
	Meals							
	Bedtime							
	Other							

WEEK TWO
Eliminate the Roadblocks

Introduction

Inevitably there are going to be bumps in the road on your spiritual journey, and sometimes these bumps will turn into roadblocks that need to be overcome. Some roadblocks require you to take a detour to get to your destination, whereas at other roadblocks the best strategy may be to gain speed and bust on through.

As you begin your second week of daily devotions, how has your journey been going? Have you settled into a routine that works for you? What seems to be the biggest obstacle for you in moving toward a closer relationship with God? Is it that you feel overwhelmed? Do you find that there are too many distractions? Are time management and procrastination problem areas for you, as they are for many Christians? Or when it comes to making time to do a daily devotion, maybe you just "don't feel like it," which is another common roadblock. This week, we will examine these and other obstacles we face in making a regular daily devotional time.

Whatever the roadblocks you may be facing, rest assured that they can be overcome, for all things are possible with God. Continue to think of devotions as a time of connecting with God. Give thanks for the progress you have made, and count your blessings as you move closer to God one day at a time. Remember that God is working within your life to help you succeed. Remember too that Jesus Christ, God's only Son, walks with you and guides you in your travels, although this may not always be apparent to you.

The Scottish writer George MacDonald explained it like this: "How often we look upon God as our last and feeblest resource! We go to Him because we have nowhere else to go. And then we learn that the storms of life have driven us, not upon the rocks, but into the desired haven."

Day One   **Feeling Overwhelmed?**

"If you have faith as small as a mustard seed, you can say to this mountain, 'Move from here to there' and it will move. Nothing will be impossible for you."
—Matthew 17:20 NIV

Everyone, at one time or another, feels overwhelmed. It's how you feel when your "to do" list is long, but your time is limited. Where do you begin? In times of crisis, it's the feeling someone has after the sudden death of a loved one. *How can I go on?* And it was the feeling of the disciples after the crucifixion of Jesus. They hid themselves in a locked room because of their fear, not knowing what to do next. They felt overwhelmed with the prospect of life without Jesus.

Uncertainty and indecision are common feelings that can also be associated with daily devotions. Like the disciples, you may wonder what to do next. Being faced with a brand-new situation or task can stop us in our tracks as we ponder our situation. Devotions may feel like an added burden, when in reality they are a tool God can use to lighten your burdens. Daily devotions are a big commitment, but the blessings far outweigh your uncertainties.

What you need to do is step out in faith.

Faith is a great weapon against uncertainty and indecision. It moves you forward. Devotions help you begin by taking a few steps toward God. Prayer is an excellent way to receive the power you need to turn inaction into daily devotions. God wants you to succeed. Faith as small as a mustard seed can move mountains, the Bible tells us. Trust God to lead you. Ask God for help. That's how to get unstuck.

A basketball star once was asked how he and his teammates overcame their fears before and during the game. He replied that it wasn't a matter of overcoming fear, but rather an exercise in fear management.

That's a key. Fear doesn't always go away, but it can be managed. The prospect of adding daily devotions to your daily routine may cause you to feel overwhelmed, or even fearful of how you will manage; but taken piece by piece, devotions are not as scary or difficult as they may initially seem. You simply need to begin and to stick with it. You can't do anything wrong when you sincerely seek a stronger relationship with God.

It has been said that good intentions don't matter much; what counts is what you get done. Forget your excuses. Get past those distractions. Force yourself past your uncertainty, whether fear-based or not, and move toward your desire to spend time with God. Do it daily. Gradually you will find daily devotions first becoming a habit, and then a blessing from God.

Now is the time to take another step in faith toward your devotional goals. Be bold. Replace uncertainty with faith. God is walking with you.

PRAYER

Dear God, thank you for helping calm my uncertainty. I want to continue daily devotions, but sometimes it seems like such a struggle. Help me move forward. Show me how to focus on you rather than on myself. Be with me today as I continue to serve you and try my best to love and serve others. Amen.

FOCUS FOR THE DAY

Today I will walk with God, taking one step at a time, and I will put my uncertainties aside.

Personal Reflection Time

Reflect on any fears and uncertainties that are holding you back from a closer relationship with God. Look at the progress you have made, and feel good about it. See how the hand of God has helped you. Think about what it means to be able to talk to God at any hour and for any reason.

Day Two   **Priorities**

Invest in truth and wisdom, discipline and good sense, / and don't part with them.
                                              —Proverbs 23:23 CEV

When it comes to finding time for daily devotions, there is not any road map that tells you how to get there. You'll need to find your own way to overcome these roadblocks, some of which may be of your own making.

The most common roadblock to doing daily devotions—making time with God a priority in your life—can be the easiest or the hardest to conquer. This roadblock is easy to break through if your greatest desire is time with God. If you don't have the desire, it is a struggle. The key is your desire.

Your day may be busy, but is it too busy to make room for God? If you are like many people, you are on the run from morning to evening, with so many places to go and so many things to do. Where does God fit into your schedule? John Bunyan has written that "he who runs from God in the morning will scarcely find him the rest of the day." There is a great deal of truth in that. Always being on the run is not conducive to having a relationship with God. You need to slow down.

If you have the desire, however, to spend ten to fifteen minutes a day with God, the secret to making it a reality is this: do it. Don't talk about it, think about it, or form a committee to explore it; simply do it. In the words of Charles Buxton, "You will never 'find' time for anything. If you want time, you must make it."

God has made you a priority. Your food, clothing, shelter, and the other necessities of life you have are blessings from God. God has given you love. God has been patient, kind, and generous with you. Add all of this up, and it's strong evidence that God wants a relationship with you. You are important to God.

How should you respond to God's love? Show love to others. Give thanks to God for all that you have been given. Go out of your way to help someone. Smile and be happy. Be a part of the church, and watch your faith grow. Be a blessing to others. But most of all, and first of all, make time for God. Make having a relationship with God your priority.

The best advice on how to begin is to begin at the beginning of your day. Carve the time out of your morning schedule. This can help provide a focus and guidance for your day. Think of it as though you are talking things over with your Boss before the business of daily life begins. Take your meeting time with God as seriously as you would regard an appointment with the most important person in the world—only your appointment is with the Creator of the Universe, the One who made you and gave you life.

With Jesus Christ as your priority, everything else in life will fall into place. Continue to "find" time for God. Ask God to help you do this. You will be blessed in your effort. That's guaranteed.

PRAYER

Dear God, thank you for making your relationship with me your priority. Help me to make the time and to take the time to get to know you better. I have so many questions to ask you, and I need your help to find my way in this life. Show me how to make you my center of the universe. Let me not waste any of the precious moments of life you have given me. Amen.

Today I will make my relationship with God my priority, and I will build my daily schedule around my friendship with Jesus.

PERSONAL REFLECTION TIME

Reflect on what is important in your life and on what is not important. Are you seeking treasure on earth or in heaven? Ask God for help in establishing your priorities.

Day Three   **Not in the Mood?**

The LORD gave this message to Jonah son of Amittai: "Get up and go to the great city of Nineveh! Announce my judgment against it because I have seen how wicked its people are." But Jonah got up and went in the opposite direction in order to get away from the LORD. He went down to the seacoast, to the port of Joppa, where he found a ship leaving for Tarshish. He bought a ticket and went on board, hoping that by going away to the west he could escape from the LORD.

—Jonah 1:1-3 NLT

I just don't feel like it today. Do I really have to? Why do I have to do this now?

Have you ever had similar thoughts or feelings? Jonah did not feel like doing what God asked him to do. In fact, he was outright defiant. God asked him to travel to Ninevah to deliver a message in person, "but Jonah got up and went in the opposite direction" (Jonah 1:3 NLT). Not only did Jonah go in the opposite direction, he also took off running. He boarded a ship to "escape from the LORD."

If you haven't discovered it already, sooner or later you'll find yourself saying, "I don't feel like reading the Bible today. I'm not up to doing a devotion or talking to God this morning." For one reason or another, you won't feel like spending time with God. Perhaps it's due to a lack of sleep or energy. Maybe you just don't feel like you have the time.

Perhaps you've done something you're ashamed of and don't want to admit it to God. Or maybe you feel like nothing is happening during your devotions. Whatever the reason might be, you want to skip out on your devotional time because you just "don't feel like it." In short, you want to turn the other way and take off, just like Jonah.

If you feel this way, believe it or not, chances are that something is working. When you don't want to meet with God, chances are that something is happening underneath the surface, and that you really do understand the importance of spending time with God. There may be times when our feelings get in the way, times when we look for excuses and try to put God off. But like going to school or to work every day, or taking care of the kids, or working out difficulties in a marriage or another relationship, we stay involved day in and day out because we've made a commitment, even though the easiest thing at the time could be to run away.

Jonah did not run away from God for long. We see in the rest of the story how God used a group of unbelieving sailors, a huge fish, and an odd plant to help Jonah realize the extravagant love of God that simply will not give up on people. Whether we like it or not, God will continue to love us. And whether we feel like it or not, God will continue to work in our lives despite our best attempts to run away.

PRAYER

Lord, thank you for loving me despite my shortcomings and my excuses to keep my distance from you. Thank you for caring for me always, even when I do not feel like returning your love. Amen.

Today I will remember that whether I feel like it or not, God can still work in my life.

List at least three things you do every day that you do not enjoy doing. Why do you do them? Think of a time when you did not feel like loving God or a time when you wanted to distance yourself from God. What happened? Do you believe God can still work in our lives even if we don't feel like he is? Why or why not?

Day Four   **Procrastination**

Children, you show love for others by truly helping them, and not merely by talking about it.
                                                —1 John 3:18 CEV

William Cowper called it "doing nothing with a great deal of skill." He was referring to the problem of procrastination, the thief who steals our time and opportunities. Procrastination is yet another roadblock on the road to spending some quality time with God each day. It's a dangerous foe, mostly because it seems so innocent.

The urge to put a task off until tomorrow or next week is common to us all. No one is immune. *One more day won't hurt. One more day won't hurt. One more day won't hurt,* we continue to tell ourselves—and soon the task has been forgotten. You never get around to what you intended to do, and an opportunity is missed. Procrastination is certainly one of life's great illusionists; it makes accomplishments disappear.

Jesus, who didn't procrastinate, can serve as an example for us all. He took immediate action to heal the sick and to demonstrate the power of love. Jesus knew that often a neglected opportunity never comes back, and he didn't have time to waste. To love someone tomorrow or forgive someone next week is not a viable option. It's dangerous to put your faith in tomorrow. It's wiser to put your faith in God today.

So putting off that daily devotional time for another day isn't the best idea. We need God every day. Consistency in devotions generates results. Trying to build a strong relationship with God through occasional conversations is a difficult task. To neglect God for a day is to break a lifeline to heaven. And the real danger is the question of how long it might be before that lifeline gets repaired.

It has been said that the present is just that, a present from God. We are promised today, not tomorrow. The Bible even warns us about planning too much into the future. It's all because God wants us to focus on today. Often, even that is more than we can handle.

Take the opportunity to enjoy today. Talk to your Creator. Share the love of God with others. Today is one of the many gifts that God has given you, along with life itself. Make the most of it. And forget about tomorrow.

PRAYER

Dear God, thank you for all of the opportunities you have given me. I am sorry if I have let procrastination delay me in being a blessing to others. Grant that I may be a responsive and responsible follower of Jesus, and take my faith seriously. I want to build a strong relationship with you. Show me the way. Amen.

Today I will be an active follower of Jesus, and I will take advantage of chances to minister to others.

PERSONAL REFLECTION TIME

Reflect upon the causes that prevent you from taking action at times. Is it fear? laziness? not wanting to get involved? or a lack of faith? Consider what you want to accomplish *today,* and also look at what you have put on the back burner. Think about how you can be God's hands, ears, and feet today as you minister to others.

Day Five   **Time Management**

The next morning Jesus awoke long before daybreak and went out alone into the wilderness to pray.
—Mark 1:35 NLT

The things we put our time into are the things that are important to us. Think about it. We make choices every day about how we will spend our time. We do the things that are important to us, as well as some things that we'd rather not do.

We go to work, we eat, we get into the car or on the bus and drive or ride, we take time to dress and get ready for the day, we sleep, we talk on the phone, we floss our teeth (though not as often as the dentist would like us to), we shop for food and clothes, we watch TV, we try to work out, we feed the cat or dog, we clean the house, we cook, and we spend time with family or friends. Every activity we do, whether we believe it or not, reflects a choice in how we spend our time. You can decide *not* to do any of the above and save time (although there would, of course, be consequences). Yes, there are exceptions, but how we spend our minutes comes down to us. We make the final choices.

The same is true about making time to spend with God. And indeed, in the midst of our busy schedules, we do need to "make" time for God. It doesn't come easily. Here are a few suggestions to help you with your decision to spend more time with God.

Schedule time with God as an appointment.

First, decide upon a specific daily time you want to spend with God. Is it in the morning? the afternoon? the evening? just before you go to sleep? Write this time down in your appointment book or calendar just as you would a doctor's appointment. This not only will remind you of your meeting with God, it also shows that this is an important commitment you have made, a priority that you've decided to give time to.

Replace another activity with devotional time.

For many people with jam-packed calendars, it may be hard to "find" more time in their day. If this is the case for you, replace all or part of an activity you currently are doing. For example, go to bed fifteen minutes later or get up fifteen minutes earlier. Take fifteen minutes from your lunch break or borrow time from shorter daily breaks. Watch fifteen minutes less of the news. Shower at night instead of in the morning, and use the time in the morning to be with God. You might even ask someone close to you for suggestions about where you might replace an activity in the course of your day.

Combine an activity with your devotional time.

Add your time of reading or reflection or prayer in with something else you are doing where possible. During breakfast, for instance, while you are eating your toast and drinking your coffee, read the Bible at the kitchen table or in your favorite reading chair. Put on your headphones and listen to an audio version of Scripture while you are walking the dog or commuting to work. As you are working out on the treadmill, put the Bible on the stand in front of you and turn off the TV. Keep a Bible in the car to read while you are waiting to pick up kids or friends.

Finding time with God is a very intentional activity, especially at first when you are working on making it a habit. But the effort is well worth it, and you will find your own rewards in the comfort and solace of God's presence and peace.

PRAYER

Lord, thank you for helping me find time to spend with you each day. And thank you for always being there with me, no matter what time of the day it is. Amen.

FOCUS FOR THE DAY

Today I will make time to spend with God.

PERSONAL REFLECTION TIME

Think of a favorite activity you've done in the past. How did you make time to do it? What did you give up or add to your schedule? Where can you combine or replace an activity to make time to spend with God?

Day Six   **Finding a Place for God**

I look to the hills! Where will I find help? / It will come from the LORD, / who created the heavens and the earth.
—Psalm 121:1-2 CEV

Have you ever noticed where country churches are located? Often they are built on tops of hills, so that they can be seen for miles around.

The people of Israel, God's chosen people, also built their places of worship on hilltops. In fact, the city of Jerusalem—the location of the Temple, the Israelites' major center of worship—is built upon hills, and you can see it for miles around. Fifteen psalms in the Bible, Psalms 120 through 134, are each called "A Song of Ascents." It is said that these were actually songs sung by worshipers on their annual trip to Jerusalem as they were going up, or ascending, the surrounding foothills of Jerusalem.

Other places of worship were also built upon hills. This may well be why the psalmist says, "I look to the hills! Where will I find help? / It will come from the LORD, / who created the heavens and the earth" (Psalm 121:1-2 CEV). God's people in the Old Testament associated God's presence with their places of worship built upon the hills.

Today you can find churches and people worshiping God in many different places, including drive-in theaters, school cafeterias, movie theaters, basements of buildings, and people's homes. While God certainly is not confined to a particular location, the places we choose for worship can help us focus our attention and emotions in order to make our meeting times with God more meaningful.

The same is true at home when we take time to meet with God. The place and environment we choose can help or hinder our time with God. As with meeting a friend for a cup of coffee or dinner, we want to choose an environment for our time with God that will add to the mood and the purpose of the meeting. For example, lights can be dim or bright, music soft or loud, and the atmosphere quaint or contemporary or unique.

When finding a place for your devotions, try to make sure that it is quiet, personalized, and consistent. A quiet space helps you to relax, to slow down, and to listen to

God. A personalized space—one you've made your own or that reflects your personality—helps you feel comfortable, secure, and at ease. A consistent space—one that you use regularly—will help you make this time you spend with God become a habit. Where will you find such a space?

Perhaps you will find it by plopping yourself down in a favorite lounge chair, or by finding a comfortable area on the porch or balcony, or by locating a nice, sunny spot by the window or outside in the yard; or perhaps it will require curling up by the fire with your favorite blanket, sequestering yourself in a quiet room of the house or office, or just finding an empty seat at the local coffee shop. Wherever it is, find a place where you can relax, shut out the rest of the world, and take some time to listen to God.

PRAYER

I thank you, Lord, for helping me find a space to enjoy your presence. Wherever that might be, help me relax so that I may grow in your love.

FOCUS FOR THE DAY

Today I will find a place where I can spend some time with God.

PERSONAL REFLECTION TIME

Where have you enjoyed spending time with God in the past? Where is your favorite spot in your house or apartment? If there currently isn't an inviting space, could you add a light, a candle, a chair, or a desk somewhere to make an existing space feel more comfortable to you? Where do your friends or family members like to spend time with God?

Day Seven   **Distractions**

He [Jesus] came back and found them asleep; and he said to
Peter, 'Asleep, Simon? Were you not able to stay awake for one
hour? Stay awake, all of you; and pray that you may be spared
the test. The spirit is willing, but the flesh is weak.' Once more he
went away and prayed. On his return he found them asleep
again, for their eyes were heavy; and they did not know how to
answer him.

—Mark 14:37-40 NEB

The Mount of Olives slopes gently upward as it climbs
east, away from Jerusalem, and there, near its foot, lies
Gethsemane. As the name of the mount indicates, stands of
olive trees dot the landscape, and in the moonlight it
becomes an eerie mix of shadow and movement. This is
where we find Jesus just a few hours before his arrest and
crucifixion. With Jesus in "horror and dismay" (Mark 14:33
NEB), the disciples fall asleep just when Jesus needs them
most. Peter, who moments before swore he would not fall
away (verse 29), falls into a deep slumber along with James
and John, not just once, the Bible says, but three times.

Let's face it. There are going to be times when you are
doing your devotions that you will lapse, times when you will
become distracted, times when you are simply unable to give
one hundred percent of your attention to the task at hand. A
lack of sleep, things to do, an argument with a spouse or
friend, bills that need to be paid, new shoes for the children,
a car that needs to be repaired, in-laws who will be spending
the next week with you, upcoming meetings or assignments
at work or at school—any of these is able to take your attention and focus away from your time with God. In fact, you
may find, like Peter, that the time of your greatest resolve to
follow Jesus is the time when you will be distracted the most.

Here are a few things you can do when distractions
arise:

1. Remember your main goal—to spend more time with God—and get back to it as quickly as possible. To paraphrase Martin Luther, the sixteenth-century reformer, you can't keep a bird from flying overhead, but you can keep it from building a nest in your hair. In other words, you can't stop every distraction from coming at you, but you can decide how you will deal with it. So decide to move on, and get back to your time with God.

2. Keep a pad and pencil at your side. If you think of something that has to be done for the day or an issue you have to deal with, write it down so you can deal with it after your devotional time is done.

3. Turn the distraction into a prayer. For example, if you suddenly think of a meeting at work that you are unprepared for, you simply can pray, "Lord, please help me be prepared for my meeting today. Help me get the information I need in a timely manner." Or if you remember a sin—something you shouldn't have done or said, pray, "Forgive me, Lord, for _____. Amen."

4. Remember that you are human. You cannot perfectly attend to every detail at all times, nor are you expected to do so. If you see a spot of dirt on the carpet and suddenly find yourself vacuuming and shampooing the entire room, instead of condemning yourself, forget about it and come back to your time with God.

Even if we "fall asleep" or become distracted, God knows our heart and will help us grow in our faith. In short, let God help you take care of each distraction as it arises, and cut yourself some slack.

PRAYER

Dear God, please take care of any distractions I might have today. Help me always come back to you and your love. Amen.

FOCUS FOR THE DAY

Today I will let God help me deal with any distractions that come my way.

PERSONAL REFLECTION TIME

What distractions have you had during the first two weeks of spending regular daily time with God? What is the hardest distraction for you to overcome? What works for you in dealing with distractions? What doesn't work? Which of the suggestions above will you try the next time you are distracted?

How Are Things Going?
Week Two

Filling in the Chart

DAILY DEVOTIONS

As in Week One, record the date for each day of the week, then make a check mark in the box for each section of the daily devotion you complete, including Scripture, Devotion, Prayer, Focus for the Day, and Personal Reflection Time. Don't worry about leaving blank spaces on the chart, but do try to get at least one check mark per day. If you happen to miss a day, simply fill in the date when you get to the next day's devotion.

This chart is not a test, where every blank must be filled in. Rather, it is a way for you to see that you are making progress in spending time with God on a daily basis, however that may happen. Lastly, give thanks for every check mark you see, and look forward to your next meeting with God.

DAILY PRAYERS

Use the Daily Prayers section of the chart to track your prayer consistency. The goal here isn't to have a check mark in every box, but to develop intentional times throughout the day when you spend time talking with God in prayer.

		Sun	Mon	Tues	Wed	Thurs	Fri	Sat
Daily Devotion	Date							
	Scripture							
	Devotion							
	Prayer							
	Focus for the Day							
	Reflection Time							
Daily Prayers	Morning							
	Meals							
	Bedtime							
	Other							

WEEK THREE
Listening to What God Is Saying

Introduction

C an God really speak to us? And if so, then how? How
do we know what God is saying? And how do we
know that it is, in fact, *God* speaking to us, and not
just something we want to hear?

God is speaking to us all the time—through the Bible,
through the work of the Holy Spirit, and through other
people. The trouble is, most of us are not listening. We
have not trained ourselves to pick out what God is saying
to us from the rest of the jumbled clattering around us.
Like trying to tune in to a radio station for better reception
as we travel down the road, we hear pieces of what God is
saying to us, but we find it difficult to hear the message
clearly.

This week, we will help you explore different ways to listen to what God is saying, so that you then will be able to
respond in the way God hopes you will. Some of the suggestions we have for you may work better than others;
some may not work at all—at least at first. But with
patience, practice, and time, and perhaps a little improvi-
sation, you will become more attuned to the task of listening and hearing what God is saying to you.

Day One   **Hearing or Listening?**

*Now the LORD came and stood there, calling as before, "Samuel!
Samuel!" And Samuel said, "Speak, for your servant is listening."*
                                                    —1 Samuel 3:10 NRSV

When it comes to listening, we can't learn a lot from insects. Most insects do not have ears. They can't "hear" like we do. Instead, God gave many insects feelers or membranes that vibrate when the insect comes in contact with sound waves from a nearby noise. This is one way in which insects know when danger is at hand. And that helps them survive.

As we begin our focus this week on listening *to* God, the good news is that, unlike most insects, we actually have ears with which to hear. This enables us to communicate with anyone we desire. Hearing permits us to understand and respond to those around us. Our ears also protect us. They can warn us about trouble. We can hear good news and bad news. Ears deliver sources of pleasure as well as pain. They are quite a gift from God, considering all the work that they do.

We can use our ears to communicate with others and with God. Often God uses other people to get his message across to us. Most people do not hear directly from God in the same way that a friend may talk to them. But God does speak to us through the Bible, through sermons, and through hymns, as well as through the touch of a friend's hand when we are feeling bad. God has no limits when it comes to trying to get through to us.

There is a difference, however, between hearing and listening. Hearing involves being aware of sounds, while listening means absorbing the message you hear. It's much easier to hear than it is to listen, especially where God is concerned. We hear sermons, but do we really *listen* to the voice of God? We hear about human need, but often we fail to *listen* to it—to absorb the meaning of the need, and respond.

The truth is, we mostly hear just what we want to hear. The end result is that our selective hearing separates us from God. We hear God just fine, but then we avoid doing what God asks of us. The message, as they say, goes in one ear and out the other.

Listening begins with our attitude toward God. If God is our priority, our Boss, this makes it much easier to communicate. It is our attitude that determines how God's message is received, and how we respond. God hears our thoughts and our prayers. God listens to us. It is the degree to which we take God seriously—as seriously as God takes us—that we are able to have a relationship with him. And having a relationship means giving and receiving, hearing and listening. Often this is a matter of us keeping up our end of the bargain.

God loves us. That makes a big difference when it comes to communication. God longs to hear from us. Because of God's love, we are always welcomed into God's kingdom, in spite of our listening deficiencies. God's love sustains us when the world's noise distracts us from our mission. Love opens our ears. It helps us listen to our Creator.

Listen to God this week. Make an extra effort. Use your devotional time to reflect on how God is speaking to you. Open your eyes and ears to the many opportunities God has placed before you. Believe that God speaks to you each day, even if you can't always hear. And always remember that God hears—and *listens*—with love.

PRAYER

Dear God, thank you for giving us the ability to listen to you and to others. Open my eyes and ears to those in need. Help me develop a good listening attitude. I need to hear your words of love and forgiveness. May I focus on listening to you this week and on making my relationship with you my top priority. Amen.

FOCUS FOR THE DAY

Today I will listen to God with my ears and with my heart.

Reflect upon what it means to be a good listener. How can you improve your ability to listen to God? How has God spoken to you in the past? How might God be speaking to you today? Consider the connection between love and listening.

Day Two   **How God Speaks to Us**

"One does not live by bread alone, / but by every word that comes from the mouth of God."

—Matthew 4:4 NRSV

The story is told of two shoppers in a grocery store who were in search of the perfect watermelon. Not just any watermelon would do; the two women were looking for the best and tastiest watermelon in the store. The pair spent a great deal of time thumping each watermelon with their knuckles. They thumped and they thumped, until one woman turned to the other and asked, "What are we listening for?"

That's a good question to ask in many situations, but especially when it comes to God. *What does God want me to know? How will I know that the message is from God?* And sometimes you may even have thought to ask, *Why can't God be plain and specific about what he wants me to do?* Wouldn't it be simpler if an e-mail with instructions from God popped up each morning on your computer screen?

God does speak to us each day, but we don't always get the message. Often this is because God speaks to us in a small voice, and we have to listen carefully in order to absorb his Word. God usually doesn't use a megaphone to blast his message at you. Skywriting isn't his style either.

Force is not God's power of choice. God's power of choice is love. God knocks softly at the door to our hearts. He waits in patience for us to respond. Jesus Christ the Son seeks to be the focus of our lives through our own free will.

It is by choice that we listen to God. And often God's message *does* get through to us. It overcomes the obstacles of our own creation, along with the distractions of this world, and the Word hits the target of a human heart. It may be that hymn during a Sunday church service that mysteriously conveys to us what we need to hear at this moment in our life. It could be a single sentence or thought from a sermon that has the same effect. The church has always been a place where God successfully plants seeds.

People—those you know and complete strangers—are also God's messengers to us. Perhaps it is the fellowship within a small-group Bible study that triggers a reaction from you. Many times it is a family member or a friend who reminds you of an important truth. That "down-on-his-luck" person you see on the corner might just direct your attention toward a ministry opportunity with people who need help. And that elderly neighbor may be pointing you toward taking the time to listen to and talk with some lonely people in the world.

Perhaps it is the *written* word, a story in a newspaper or magazine that God uses to send you in a new direction. Daily devotions and Bible meditations also have been known to launch new awareness and fresh starts. There could even be a billboard that opens our eyes or our hearts. Or maybe it's a movie, a play, a television program, or the evening news that God enlists as his messenger. Do the math; there are endless possibilities.

Remember that certain "coincidence"? Maybe it was something a bit more than just random fate. God does work in mysterious ways, you know. The Lord even has been known to use angels in disguise to nudge us in the right direction.

God may be speaking to you right now. Perhaps you will receive a message from the Lord today. Watch for it. Open your ears and your eyes. God has something to say to you!

PRAYER

Dear God, thank you for your words of direction, comfort, encouragement, and love. Forgive me for not listening at times, and for tossing away or failing to recognize the message or the messenger. Grant me the wisdom to distinguish your often small and quiet voice in this noisy and chaotic world. Amen.

FOCUS FOR THE DAY

Today I will be open to receiving messages from God.

PERSONAL REFLECTION TIME

Reflect on how God has spoken to you in the past. Think about how you have responded and why. Are you open to the challenges God may place before you?

Day Three   **Receptive Body Language**

"And when thou prayest, thou shalt not be as the hypocrites are: for they love to pray standing in the synagogues and in the corners of the streets, that they may be seen of men. Verily I say unto you, They have their reward. But thou, when thou prayest, enter into thy closet, and when thou hast shut thy door, pray to thy Father which is in secret; and thy Father which seeth in secret shall reward thee openly."

—Matthew 6:5-6 KJV

In Week Two we mentioned that the *place* where you choose to spend time with God can make a difference in terms of how well you are able to hear God speaking. Perhaps at first glance, the passage in Matthew 6:5-6 may seem as though it is suggesting a place to pray. But before you start cleaning out your closets looking for enough space to sit down to pray, know that Jesus is talking about the *attitude* people adopt when they pray. Rather than praying in order to call attention to ourselves and to gain self-approval, as Jesus says the hypocrites do, when we pray we should give all of our attention to the Father. Our attitude and our receptiveness to God when we pray can make a difference in how we communicate with God.

There are several things you can do when praying that can help you to be more open and receptive to God. At the same time, these things will allow you to follow Jesus' advice about focusing your attention on God rather than on yourself. First, try to begin with a "quiet body." Sit down, relax, and take a few deep breaths, letting the air come in and go out slowly. Close your eyes. Empty your mind of thoughts, and mentally slow down. Like being in a closet, try to close out all outside distractions. Try to keep your legs positioned comfortably with both feet flat on the floor, and with your back straight but not rigid. Let your arms rest lightly upon your thighs or on the arms of a chair, with your palms open and facing upward, toward heaven. Hands in an open, upward position are receptive to God. Sit quietly, and wait.

As the psalmist says, "Be still before the LORD and wait patiently for him" (Psalm 37:7 NIV). Listen for what God is saying to you. It might come in a thought; it might come in a picture; it might simply be "white space" that you see in your mind. The important thing is that you are open and receptive to God's message. Like a vessel being filled, you are God's vessel waiting to be filled with God's spirit and peace.

You may not be aware of anything happening the first few times you practice this particular body language of prayer, but know that in time, as you keep yourself open to God's voice, God will speak to you in a way you understand.

PRAYER

Dear God, help me to be open and receptive to you when I pray. Help me focus my attention on what you can do, rather than what I can do. Amen.

FOCUS FOR THE DAY

Today I will be an open vessel that God can fill.

PERSONAL REFLECTION TIME

Do you believe the suggestions above for keeping yourself open and receptive to God in terms of body language will help or hinder you? Have you tried them yet? If so, what worked? What didn't work? Are there other ways in which you physically can make yourself more open to hearing and receiving God's Word?

Day Four   Intuition

Answer me quickly, O LORD;
my spirit fails.
Do not hide your face from me,
or I shall be like those who go down to the Pit.
Let me hear of your steadfast love in the morning,
for in you I put my trust.
Teach me the way I should go,
for to you I lift up my soul.
Save me, O LORD, from my enemies;

I have fled to you for refuge.
Teach me to do your will,
for you are my God.
Let your good spirit lead me
on a level path.

—Psalm 143:7-10 NRSV

Someone once said that the height of mental activity occurs between the ages of four and eighteen: At age four we seem to know all of the questions, and at age eighteen we seem to know all of the answers!

When listening to God, however, not everything is packaged neatly in questions and answers. There are times when we think we hear God speaking to us in clear, certain terms; but often the message comes as more of a nudge, a gnawing feeling, a gut reaction, or an intuition rather than a definite yes or no. And it might not come all at once; the answer may come over days or weeks or months or even years, in bits and pieces of information.

A youth worker in a church was looking to make a career change. While she always had dreamed of being a writer, she never really had pursued a job in the writing or publishing field. On a whim she called the publishing house of her church denomination. As it turned out, they had an entry-level editing position open, and she was qualified; they would call her back about an interview. Unfortunately, however, they called back to tell her that the position had just been filled. Didn't God want her to leave youth work? Was her hope to become a writer just a silly idea after all?

Three months later, still thinking about her dream to work with words, the woman felt the desire to contact the publishing house again. Why? She wasn't sure. This time, though, the publishing house had a different position open, one that required the advanced theological training she already had acquired at the seminary. The salary was also quite a bit higher. She interviewed for the position and got it. Three weeks later, she was working in a position she had only dreamed about months before.

Intuition has gotten a bad rap over the years. People often think of it as a silly feeling or a decision pulled out of the air based on nothing more than happenstance. Today, however, science has taught us just the opposite. Rather than being a feeling out of nowhere, intuition is based on every life experience you've ever had. When you get a "funny feeling" about something, it is likely that your brain and your senses have picked up on something they've experienced before. Based on past events, your mind is evaluating all of the possibilities in light of the current situation. For example, if your intuition tells you you're in danger, your mind, body, and senses probably are picking up signals from your environment that have signaled danger in the past.

The same is true in our prayer lives. God speaks to us in many ways. When we have "a hunch" or suddenly think of something we ought to do, it could be God's Spirit guiding us in the direction we should go. As the psalmist says, "Let your good spirit lead me."

PRAYER

Dear Lord, help me keep my life and all possibilities open to you. Help me hear all of the ways in which you speak to me, as your Spirit guides me. Amen.

FOCUS FOR THE DAY

Today I will pay attention to my intuition.

PERSONAL REFLECTION TIME

Has there ever been a time when your intuition turned out to be correct? What happened? Have you ever experienced a time when you felt that God was nudging you to do something in your life—to make a career change, to call a friend from the past, to visit someone, or to ask someone for forgiveness? What happened? How did you know it was God speaking?

Day Five   **Focused Listening**

Jesus answered: I have explained the secrets about the kingdom of heaven to you, but not to others. Everyone who has something will be given more. But people who don't have anything will lose even what little they have. I use stories when I speak to them because when they look, they cannot see, and when they listen, they cannot hear or understand. . . . But God has blessed you, because your eyes can see and your ears can hear!
                                —Matthew 13:11-13, 16 CEV

The man was complaining to his friend that his wife got angry at him for not listening to her. "Well, what exactly did she say?" asked the friend. "I don't know," the man said. "I can't remember."

Much of this week's focus has centered on being intentional about listening to God. That one suggestion—being intentional—if taken seriously, can make the difference between just hearing God and really understanding what God is saying to you.

Morton Kelsey, a Catholic theologian who has a heart for hearing God's voice, notes that we are bombarded by thousands and thousands of messages daily from the world around us. In fact, we receive so many messages and stimuli to our brain on a daily basis that we easily could be overwhelmed, unable to carry out the simplest tasks. The brain, however, has a tremendous capability of picking out only the most important things we need to focus on at any given time. By limiting what we take in, we are able to better focus on what needs to be done.

The same thing is true when listening to God. Oftentimes we don't need more input, we need to limit the input. Like picking out new carpet or paint for a bedroom, having a hundred different options at first doesn't always make things easier. After we weed out the majority of colors we don't like, however, it's much easier to make a decision based on two or three choices. By limiting our choices and being selective about what we focus on, it is easier to make a decision. So, too, limiting what we hear from the outside world allows us to pick up the voice of God. Like the disciples, God has blessed us with eyes that can see, ears that can hear, and a mind that can process information and comprehend. The key, however, is to be selective.

During your devotional time, you may want to be selective in what you read. Instead of reading an entire chapter of Scripture, try focusing on a few verses. The Benedictine priests encourage focusing on just one or two words during meditation. As you read your devotion, what word stands out for you from all the rest? When a word seems to "jump off the page," stop and ask yourself, *Why is this word important? What is God trying to say to me?* When you pray, instead of compelling yourself to pray a long, drawn-out prayer, focus on one person or one need. Visualize the need, see the person in your mind, and simply recite the person's name. When you are in church listening to the sermon, wait expectantly to hear the few key words God is speaking to you. What makes your heart flutter in joy, shame, or fear? What is God saying to you?

Focused, selective listening allows us to hear God's voice, even when thousands of other noises are competing for our attention. Tuning out all the other voices except God's is the first step in helping us hear and understand.

PRAYER

Dear God, give me ears to hear your message. Open my heart to your message, whatever it might be. Amen.

FOCUS FOR THE DAY

Today I will practice selective listening in order to discern how God is speaking to me.

PERSONAL REFLECTION TIME

Are there times when you "zone out" while talking to your spouse, a friend, a coworker, or your children? Why do you think this happens? In what ways can you be more intentional about filtering out excess noise and really listening to God during your devotional time? during your time at church? throughout your day?

Day Six   **When God Is Silent**

God has given us his Spirit. That is how we know that we are one with him, just as he is one with us.
—1 John 4:13 CEV

Peter was saying his bedtime prayers when he noticed his sister also kneeling by her bed with the same activity in mind. Peter yelled over to her, "The line's busy! *I'm* talking to him! Wait your turn!"

It's not funny when we can't seem to get through to God. It feels like we get a busy signal or get put on hold. Try as we might, God seems elusive to us. He is in heaven, while we are on earth, unsuccessfully attempting to start a long-distance conversation. It's not like we dialed the wrong number, or that God has turned his cell phone off. We know God is there. He's just not responding. Or so it seems.

"My God, why have you forgotten me?" is a question that every believer has asked at one time or another. During such a time, we feel as if we have been abandoned by God. It is frustrating. Our minds cannot understand why God won't answer our prayers. We don't feel God's presence. We only feel alone.

In times like these, it can be helpful to remember what we do know about God. We can recall his promises to his followers. The Bible tells us that the Lord is always near. Jesus loves us. Nothing can snatch us out of his hand. God has a long, long history of being there for us and all believers. His track record is perfect. Why doubt him now?

When God seems far away, we can also recall how God has blessed us. We can give thanks for the times when we have felt God's close presence. We can look back on times of trouble when God has saved us, healed us, and answered our prayers. The goodness of God is a constant. If God was with us yesterday, he is certainly with us today. Have faith, and continue to believe.

God has a plan for everyone, for each one of us, even when God seems to be silent. Maybe the answer to our prayer is to be patient and wait. Maybe God is saying that we need a time of silence and reflection. Maybe this is not the right time or place for our request. Could it be that God is saying *no* to us, and we are unwilling or unable to accept that? Perhaps we need to be humbled. So we wait.

There is one certainty: Sooner or later, God will answer. You will feel his presence again. It will seem just like old times. This will be because you continued to seek God. And eventually you may discover that God really was not out of reach after all, and that there was a reason God seemed far away. God knows best. Sometimes, that's all we need to know.

PRAYER

Dear God, thank you for being a constant in my life. Even when I don't feel your presence, I know that you are nearby. Forgive me for straying. Often I am the one who is distant. Help me continue to have faith and believe in you. Amen.

FOCUS FOR THE DAY

Today I will believe in the nearness of God. I will live by faith.

PERSONAL REFLECTION TIME

Reflect on how close you feel to God. In what past situations have you felt the presence of God? How has God been a friend to you? What expectations do you have when you pray to God? Examine possible reasons God may seem distant from you at times.

Day Seven   **When God Answers**

My God, my God, why have you forsaken me?
Why are you so far from saving me,
so far from the words of my groaning?
O my God, I cry out by day, but you do not answer,
by night, and am not silent.

Yet you are enthroned as the Holy One;
you are the praise of Israel.
In you our fathers put their trust;
they trusted and you delivered them.
They cried to you and were saved;
in you they trusted and were not disappointed.
                                        —Psalm 22:1-5 NIV

A man was talking to God one day and said, "Is it true that a million years is like a second to you?" God said, "Yes, that is true." So the man asked, "Well, then, is it also true that a million dollars is like a penny to you?" And God's reply was, "Yes, that is true as well." The man continued innocently, saying, "Well, then, could I please have a penny?" And God, with wisdom and understanding, said, "Just a second."

It doesn't take long to figure out, especially if we are spending time with God on a regular basis, that God's answers to our prayers do not always come overnight. Or the next day. Or the day after that. In fact, some of God's answers don't come for years, and perhaps some will never come in our lifetime. A life spent listening to God is often a life of waiting, and we soon discover that God's timeline often is very different from our own. We want it now, even though God's answer might be "Just a second." It's enough to get you to wonder whether God is really listening to you.

Does God really hear our prayer? It's the same question posed by the psalmist: "O my God, I cry out by day, but you do not answer, / by night, and am not silent" (Psalm 22:2 NIV). Why doesn't God answer us in our time of need?

I'm sure Jesus was wondering the same thing in his desperate hour of need. On the cross, crucified with nails driven through his hands and feet, a crown of thorns embedded into his skull, his body torn open hours before with whips containing bits of glass and metal in the leather strips. Hanging on the cross, he mouthed these very words: "My God, my God, why have you forsaken me?" (Matthew 27:46; Mark 15:34 NRSV). And even to his Son, God replies with silence. There is no answer.

Of course, we all know what happened to Jesus after his death on Good Friday, and if we fast-forward a few days we see God's response in raising Jesus from the dead. There is an answer after all, but there was waiting in between.

Answers to prayer will come, but they will come in God's time, not our time. We'd like them to come in a second, but the answer can seem to take a million years! Who has that kind of time to wait?

The psalmist, like us, seems a little impatient: "Why are you so far from saving me, / so far from the words of my groaning?" (verse 1*b*). But ultimately, the psalmist knows that God's steadfastness has been proven time and time again: "In you our fathers put their trust; / they trusted and you delivered them. / They cried to you and were saved; / in you they trusted and were not disappointed" (verses 4-5). This is why the psalmist can cry out to God in the first place, because he or she knows that God is the only one who can do something about the request. Similarly, when we were children, we used to cry out to our parents when we wanted an answer because we knew they could deliver. Yet the answer wasn't always immediate.

Yes, God answers us. God hears our requests—all of them. The answers may not come as soon as we want, however, and they may not be the answers we expect. But they will come. God will respond, one way or another, even if it seems to us like it's taking a million years.

PRAYER

Dear Lord, thank you for hearing all of my prayers, both spoken and unspoken. Give me the trust and patience to wait for your timing rather than insisting upon my own.

FOCUS FOR THE DAY

Today I will wait for God to answer my prayers in God's time, rather than my own.

Think of a time when you waited for God to answer one of your prayers. What was the hardest part about waiting? Was the prayer eventually answered? If so, how?

How Are Things Going?
Week Three

For instructions on using the chart below, see page 31.

		Sun	Mon	Tues	Wed	Thurs	Fri	Sat
Daily Devotion	Date							
	Scripture							
	Devotion							
	Prayer							
	Focus for the Day							
	Reflection Time							
Daily Prayers	Morning							
	Meals							
	Bedtime							
	Other							

WEEK FOUR
Living Your Faith Through Action

Introduction

*Y*ou will find as you look back upon your life that the moments when you have really lived are the moments when you have done things in the spirit of love." This observation by Henry Drummond provides an excellent starting point for Week Four of your spiritual journey. It illustrates the connection between faith and action, two of the most powerful forces in the world. This week you will have the opportunity to put your faith to work by reaching out to others in a spirit of love. Where and when this will happen, only God knows. Think of it as a surprise.

You may know by now that devotions involve more than just talking to God. They often are the spark for service within your home, your church, and your community. God calls us to put our faith to work where it is needed. During his ministry, Jesus repeatedly demonstrated the power of love and faith combined. As his disciples, we are called to follow in his footsteps and to change the world by one act of love at a time.

Living your faith through action can be accomplished in a variety of ways, and each day this week we will examine a different aspect of what that means. Stepping out in faith includes how you think, what you say, what you hear, what you dream, and many other aspects of daily life. And the launching pad for your ministry will be your daily devotions. Get ready—it's going to be an amazing week!

Day One   **What You See**

Examine yourselves to see whether you are living in the faith.
                                        —2 Corinthians 13:5*a* NRSV

What do you see when you view your world through the eyes of faith? Perhaps you see an opportunity to serve others. Perhaps you see the possibilities that exist for people to walk a new path in life. As you open your eyes, the needs of this world come into sharper focus. And your faith in God encourages you to take risks as you offer a helping hand.

The eyes of faith also enable you to see Jesus. You see Jesus in the homeless person, in the prison inmate, in the hospitalized child, in the jobless woman, in the person with AIDS, and in others who need a message of hope and love. And they, in turn, may see Jesus in you.

James Russell Lowell once wrote that "all the beautiful entiments in the world weigh less than a single lovely ction." It is this thought that captures the essence of where ministry begins. It starts with a single lovely action. The eyes of faith transform good thoughts into acts of love.

To live your faith is to begin a spiritual journey that will take you to uncharted territory. "The steps of faith / Fall on he seeming void, and find / The rock beneath," observed he poet John Greenleaf Whittier. Your faith is a candle that shows you the way and lights the way for others. You walk with Jesus as his disciple.

So, what do you need to take with you on this spiritual adventure? First, take your *sensitivity*. You will need to be able to see beyond the surface and to be sensitive to the needs and feelings of others. Appearances can be deceiving; don't judge. Second, you will need to take your *work clothes;* laboring for the Lord can give you dirty hands and clothes. Good works coupled with faith mean plenty of activity. And finally, bring along your *trust*. To trust is to put your faith in the power of God. Trust in the Lord, believe in yourself, and trust that you will be provided with all you need to complete the tasks at hand.

George Eliot (the pen name of English novelist Mary Ann Evans) asked the question, "What do we live for, if it is not to make life less difficult to each other?" That is the question each of us must answer. Faith, combined with action, is certainly a key to leaving your world a little bit better than you found it. Open your eyes; there's a lot to be done.

PRAYER

Dear God, my eyes see needs all around me, and yet sometimes I look the other way. Give me eyes of faith and a heart that believes that, through you, I can accomplish any task you give me. Thank you for the many blessings you have given me. May I now be a blessing to others. Grant me this opportunity. Amen.

FOCUS FOR THE DAY

Today I will open my eyes to a world that needs me.

PERSONAL REFLECTION TIME

Reflect on how the gift of sight can be used as a tool for ministry. Think about how employing your faith can change someone's life through seeing a need and acting on it. Contemplate your gifts, as well as how you can use them to bless others.

Day Two   **What You Say**

"The farmer I talked about is anyone who brings God's message to others, trying to plant good seed within their lives."
—Mark 4:14 TLB

Some people talk to their plants. That may seem a bit strange, but studies have shown that plants respond positively to kind words and attention. They thrive on love, praise, and water. On the other hand, plants that are ignored often struggle to survive. Perhaps plants have a great deal in common with people when it comes to the spoken word.

If human words can cause plants to thrive or barely survive, think of the power words can have on other human beings! Words can make you laugh or cry. They can build up or take you down. God created words to be tools ne sentence at a time, may build a better world.

The sentences "I love you" and "I hate you" illustrate the potential of the spoken word to bring pleasure or pain. Used for evil, words can take over a life like weeds in a garden. Words of hate, words of fear, words of prejudice, and words of profanity are as dangerous as a gun in the hands of a child. They can hurt, and they can destroy. You've seen the misery words can cause.

God has given us a choice, however. Words can also be a servant. They can help people grow. Words can plant encouragement or sow seeds of love and support. They can cultivate friendships with kindness. Words can become rays of sunlight. These are the ingredients for a bumper crop of goodness. That's what God wants us to plant.

In the parable of the sower, Jesus talks about a farmer scattering seeds. The seeds land both on rocky ground and in good soil. Words are like those seeds. Some words generate a plentiful harvest. People hear God's message of love and forgiveness, and they are forever changed. But in order that to happen, we "farmers" of God's Word first need to t into the fields of the world and work the land. ou want to put your faith in action, begin with your language. Value your words. Talk about your faith in God. Speak the truth. Don't gossip. Show God's love by using positive words that build people up. Take time to pray. Read the Bible; it contains the Word of Life.

We are all connected by our words and actions. That's what God intended. We are meant to be the family of God. Nourish others today by what you say and by what you do. And grow where you have been planted by the Master Gardener.

PRAYER

Dear God, thank you for giving me the opportunity to speak on your behalf. May my words and actions today be pleasing to you. Help me offer words of encouragement, love, and forgiveness to others. Guide my steps so that I may continue to walk in your ways. Amen.

FOCUS FOR THE DAY

Today I will choose my words carefully and sow seeds of God's love.

PERSONAL REFLECTION TIME

Think about your personal vocabulary. Do your words and deeds reflect the love of God? Can people see Jesus in you when they hear what you have to say?

Day Three   **What You Hear**

Listen! For I will speak clearly, / you will have plain speech from me; / for I speak nothing but truth / and my lips detest wicked talk.
                                                        —Proverbs 8:6-7 NEB

Helen Miller had enjoyed the Reverend Johnson's sermon so much that she couldn't wait to tell him so as she exited the church. As she shook the pastor's hand, Mrs.

Miller exclaimed, "That was a fantastic sermon! Every point you made applies to a friend or family member of mine. I can't wait to tell them!"

Although you may smile at the words of Mrs. Miller, it is no laughing matter how many of us fail to apply God's Word to our lives. The Sunday sermon is just one example of how the word of God often goes in one ear and out the other.

You know how it goes. You sit in church and listen to the sermon. The pastor makes some good points. You even agree with the message. And by the end of the service, you are out the door and back to reality. Nothing changes—it's business as usual. In your defense, you note that the pastor couldn't have been talking about *you*, as your name wasn't even mentioned in the sermon. *That* would have attracted your attention.

This sort of response is actually God's fault when you think about it: God gave us freedom of choice. Everything is optional. It's a matter of choice to read the Bible, to attend church, to help persons who are in need, to serve on a committee, to teach Sunday school, and to contribute financially.

You see, God is all about love. God loves us and desires that we respond in love. There are no hidden catches. There is no small print. Love is God's policy. It has been that way since the time of Adam and Eve. God does not change.

The choice is ours. We can listen to God and do his will, or we can pretend not to hear. The sometimes small, quiet voice of God can be drowned out if we permit it to be. We don't lose God's love if we refuse him, but we do miss a great opportunity designed just for us.

When Jesus calls us to action, sometimes there are others who could do the job. But that's not the point. Jesus wants *you*. In his plan, you are the best person for the job. You were selected. And God is waiting for your decision.

To be able to hear God is to be able to feel the tugs at our hearts. It is the love of Jesus that calls us to do the right thing. God is speaking to you today. Are you listening?

PRAYER

Dear God, forgive me for tuning you out and listening instead to other voices. Thank you for giving me ears to hear you. Open my eyes and my ears to the needs of others. Point me in the direction you want me to go, and walk with me all the days of my life. Amen.

FOCUS FOR THE DAY

Today I will tune in to God and listen throughout the day to his voice.

PERSONAL REFLECTION TIME

Reflect on your ability to hear the needs of others. Consider the connection between loving and listening. Think about how you can give the gift of being a good listener to someone today.

Day Four   **What You Think**

Hear, O Israel: The LORD our God, the LORD is one. Love the LORD your God with all your heart and with all your soul and with all your strength. These commandments that I give you today are to be upon your hearts. Impress them on your children. Talk about them when you sit at home and when you walk along the road, when you lie down and when you get up. Tie them as symbols on your hands and bind them on your foreheads. Write them on the doorframes of your houses and on your gates.
                                        —Deuteronomy 6:4-9 NIV

You are what you think. Studies have shown time and time again that what you think about has a direct influence on who you are as a person. Olympians and professional athletes call it "visualization," where they see in their mind the outcome they want to achieve. Day after day they form pictures in their minds of accomplishing their goals. It can be during a few short words they speak quietly to themselves while in the starting gate. It can be done in a few deep breaths they take to quiet their bodies down before their routines. It can be in five to ten seconds before the race, with eyes closed, when they watch the movie playing in their mind of exactly what is going to happen. Visualization works because the body will subconsciously work to fulfill the conscious goal.

You are what you think. What have you been thinking about lately? If someone played the movies in your mind for the last ten minutes, would you like what you saw on the screen? Would it represent the person you've always wanted to be and the goals you've always wanted to achieve?

You are what you think. In Deuteronomy 6:4-9, Moses is addressing the entire nation of Israel shortly before they enter into the promised land of Canaan. They are still in the wilderness, east of the Jordan River. An eleven-day journey had taken forty years for them to complete because of their disobedience (see Deuteronomy 1:2)—they had not kept their thoughts focused on God. Instead they focused on food, water, their enemies, and other gods—so God let them wander. Moses admonishes the Israelites to get back on track. God is the reason they are still alive and the reason they soon will enter into the land God has promised them. But they must be single-minded in their purpose. They must center their thoughts on God and God alone. "Love the LORD your God with all your heart and with all your soul and with all your strength. These commandments that I give you today are to be upon your hearts. Impress them on your children. Talk about them when you sit at home and when you walk along the road, when you lie down and when you get up. Tie them as symbols on your hands and bind them on your foreheads. Write them on the doorframes of your houses and on your gates" (Deuteronomy 6:5-9 NIV). In short, keep God on your mind continuously.

These verses from Deuteronomy (6:4-9) became part of the *Shema* prayer, words that the Jews were to recite every morning and evening. It was a way for them to keep God in their thoughts from when they woke until they went to sleep.

You are what you think. Committing yourself wholeheartedly to God simply means to follow the advice of Moses. Keep God's love and God's words in front of you at all times. Talk about them with your children, talk about them at home and away from home, at night and in the morning, put them on your hands, forehead, and doorframes.

You are what you think. Keep your thoughts focused on God, and let God take care of the rest.

PRAYER

Dear God, thank you for loving me enough to save me. Amidst all of life's distractions, help me focus on you. Amen.

FOCUS FOR THE DAY

Today I will think about God with all my heart, soul, and mind.

PERSONAL REFLECTION TIME

Use the Scripture for today as a list of ways you can keep focused on God. In what ways can you remember God with your heart? your soul? your strength? at home and away from home? before you go to sleep and after you wake up? In what other ways can you keep your thoughts focused on God?

Day Five   **What You Dream**

> *Take delight in the LORD,*
>   *and he will give you your heart's desires.*
> *Commit everything you do to the LORD.*
> *Trust him, and he will help you.*
>   —Psalm 37:4-5 NLT

What have you always dreamed of doing with your life?

Oftentimes we think of dreams or goals as nothing more than daydreaming, a few wispy thoughts that dissolve into thin air. But our dreams and goals are the very things that can give us life and hope and purpose. It is our dreams that can be the driving force for how we act and respond, to ourselves and to others. It is our dreams that can keep us going when no one else believes in us, and they can inspire us to forge ahead when all roads seem blocked and all doors appear closed. Our dreams can shape who we become and who we are as people, and they can define us by the values we believe in. Rather than extraneous fluff, our dreams are at the very core of our existence.

In Chaim Potok's moving novel *My Name is Asher Lev,* a young Jewish boy by the name of Asher finds within himself a love of, and a rare gift for, drawing and painting. His earliest memories center around his love, passion, and yes, even hatred for his art. He sees as no one else around him sees. He feels what others do not feel. He picks up the rhythm of the world around him. And to all of these things he gives life through his drawings and paintings. He is consumed with expressing himself through the canvas, and he is both overjoyed and repulsed by what he brings to life because of his naked honesty in how he views the world. While the people closest to him humor this "hobby" for a few years, they soon pass off his gift as a waste of time. His parents want him to do something useful with his life, like be a doctor or a lawyer or a professor. Does he do as his parents and his tradition request of him and live a miserable life? Or does he follow his God-given talent as an artist and deal with the scary, and perhaps even terrible, consequences?

What dream has God given you? What one thing pops up in the back of your mind when you don't have to be "realistic"? What would you like to do, but haven't pursued because of a lack of time, money, or resources? Do you have a desire to teach? Do you have a dream to do mission work, if only for a week, somewhere in the world? Do you feel that God is calling you to go to seminary, start an outreach group, work with married couples, respond to the needs of children in your community, or write a book? What is your dream? Have you taken it seriously?

Following your dream can take a tremendous amount of faith because the goal can appear so far out of reach. It also can be difficult because those closest to you may not feel as strongly about your dream as you do. But the great thing about accomplishing a dream is that you need God's help to do it. When something appears too far away to reach, try asking for—and then depending on—God's help.

Find your heart's desire. Then, as the psalmist urges, "Commit everything you do to the LORD. / Trust him, and he will help you." Yes, even with the dreams of your heart. *Especially* with the dreams of your heart.

PRAYER

Dear God, help me find the one thing you'd most like me to do with my life. Help me discover how I can live my life for you. Then give me the faith and the courage to do your will. Amen.

FOCUS FOR THE DAY

Today I will commit my dreams and goals to God.

When you think of your personal dreams or goals, what comes to mind? How long have you had this dream? If you can't think of a dream, what have you always wanted to do with your life? What are your strengths, gifts, and talents? How might you use your gifts for God?

Day Six   What You Have

Now God has given us many kinds of special abilities, but it is the same Holy Spirit who is the source of them all. There are different kinds of service to God, but it is the same Lord we are serving. There are many ways in which God works in our lives, but it is the same God who does the work in and through all of us who are his. The Holy Spirit displays God's power through each of us as a means of helping the entire church.

—1 Corinthians 12:4-7 TLB

W. C. Fields was a wealthy man, but just how wealthy no one will ever know. He didn't want anyone to know just how much money he had, so he came up with a plan to keep his secret.

In order to hide his wealth, the famous comic opened hundreds of bank accounts across the United States. Each account was under a false name. Only Fields knew where his money was, and unfortunately he took that information with him when he died. Executors of his estate were only able to locate fewer than fifty of his many bank accounts. It is estimated that hundreds of thousands of dollars were never found.

Fields hid his assets successfully, but that's not always a wise thing to do. His riches were lost in an effort to protect them. And yet it is surprising how often this happens to people today. The riches given by God get tucked away and forgotten. These riches come in all shapes and sizes. For example, some people have the ability to paint, others know how to build and work with machines, some are wonderfully talented as writers, and many are able to play musical instruments. These talents are gifts from God, and, as with all gifts, what you decide to do with them is completely up to you.

It is your choice: Use your talents and they increase, or hide away your skills and ideas and risk losing them. That is one reason professional athletes practice daily. They know that talent grows through practice and by using their skills. Assets increase in value through use. Practice does make perfect as skills are honed over a lifetime.

God gave you talents for a reason. You have an obligation to share them with others and to give them away. They are made for glorifying God as you use them to help people in need. Whether you sell, teach, cook, or heal, your talents, combined with the talents of others, further the kingdom of God. You are God's hands and an instrument of change as this world continues to be shaped by the power of God.

As you continue with your devotions this week, consider how you can put your faith into action by making the most of your assets. Words are great, but actions do speak louder than words. Action brings happiness to us and to others. And more important, it can deliver God's love to a love-starved world.

So think about what God has given you. Give thanks for the talent and imagination that make you unique. Use your talents so that you become a blessing to others. Minister to those who are in need. Serve those who are less fortunate. Spread your wealth around and invest it in the kingdom of God. That's the best way to gain eternal dividends on God's investment in you.

PRAYER

Dear God, thank you for the many blessings you have given me. Help me use my talents to help others. Move my feet to action, and open my eyes that I might become part of the solution to the problems of this world. May your Spirit encourage me to love others and to give more of myself. Amen.

FOCUS FOR THE DAY

Today I will seek opportunities to use my gifts to minister to others.

PERSONAL REFLECTION TIME

Reflect on the talents you have been given. Count your blessings and consider how you are using them. Have you hidden or neglected any assets? Are you using the wealth God has given you to the best advantage? Do you need to practice more? Can you use a talent you have to minister to others? What do you need to do in order to become the best you can be?

Day Seven   **What You Do**

*Ponder the path of thy feet, and let all thy ways be established. /
Turn not to the right hand nor to the left: remove thy foot from evil.*
                                                —Proverbs 4:26-27 KJV

Many years ago, newspapers carried the story of a missing boy. The question was whether the ten-year-old was abducted, lost, or a runaway. After eleven days, the boy was discovered at the World's Fair. He had grown tired of waiting for his parents to take him there, so the boy ventured out on his own. Coins from a fountain provided money for food. He slept at night in a lifeboat at one of the displays. The boy had the time of his life, although he knew he was in the wrong.

The Bible tells us about two similar stories. The parable of the prodigal son tells of a young man who flees home for high adventure, only to later return home in humility. And then there is the account of Jonah, a prophet who fled when God called upon him to perform a task and ended up in the belly of a large fish. Both accounts are of people who didn't want to be—or didn't want to go—where they belonged.

Where do I belong? This is a question all of us have asked at one time or another. We belong with God, but often our desires send us in a different direction. We flee from God, like a runaway going to the World's Fair. God wants us to take the long road of service, but instead we take the short-cut of pleasure. Maybe this is because we, like the runaway boy, get tired of waiting for promises to be fulfilled. We try to grab our own blessings. In any event, it is our own stubbornness that sets us apart from God.

Apart from God, we may pretend we are having the time of our lives, but really we are not. The happiness and adventure we seek cannot be found on our own; it is found in a close relationship with God. Obedience is the key to an active and living faith. As Jonah discovered, you can't flee from God.

God has plans for us. Those plans require our commitment and faith. It is God's desire for us to find happiness and fulfillment by serving others. God wants us to be servants. That means a life of helping people, encouraging others, giving ourselves away, and loving others whether or not they love us. It may not be easy or glamorous, but that's the calling of a Christian.

The Lord didn't put us here to run off to the fair and to ignore the needs of others. We will only find our heart's desire by staying "at home" with God. Living a rich and rewarding life of faith through action begins by staying, not by straying. Everything we seek, we already have, through Christ our Lord.

PRAYER

Dear God, I am sorry for often running away from the work you have called me to do. Forgive me for pursuing my selfish desires and thinking that I know best. Help me possess a faith that possesses me. Guide my thoughts and actions so that they may be pleasing to you. Thank you for staying near me. Amen.

FOCUS FOR THE DAY

Today I will walk hand in hand with God toward the work that needs to be done.

PERSONAL REFLECTION TIME

Reflect on what it means to be a true follower of Jesus Christ. What obstacles are preventing you from a closer relationship with God? Why are you sometimes tempted to run? Meditate on what God is calling you to do.

How Are Things Going?
Week Four

For instructions on using the chart below, see page 31.

		Sun	Mon	Tues	Wed	Thurs	Fri	Sat
Daily Devotion	Date							
	Scripture							
	Devotion							
	Prayer							
	Focus for the Day							
	Reflection Time							
Daily Prayers	Morning							
	Meals							
	Bedtime							
	Other							

WEEK FIVE
Living Your Faith in the World

Introduction

*F*aith is an action word. Without movement, without doing something, without being involved in life, faith doesn't mean much, nor does it have much of an impact on others. It isn't the thirty years of Jesus' life living at home that we remember—the Gospels tell us very little about this time. But what is important, and the stories that we remember, are the three short years of Jesus' ministry away from his home as he traveled and taught in the surrounding communities. It was through his time out in the world interacting with laborers, farmers, shepherds, and leaders in the religious, political, and military arenas that the teachings of Jesus became real for people. It was out in the world that Jesus made this loving, saving, forgiving God come to life.

This week you will be exploring different ways to live out your faith in the world. What does it mean for God to be involved in your life at home, with your extended family, in your neighborhood, in your community, at your workplace, and at church?

Faith is an action word. So get ready for some action, and be open to the many ways in which God can "rock" your world!

Day One   **At Home**

Then he returned to Nazareth with them and was obedient to them; and his mother stored all these things in her heart. So

Jesus grew both in height and in wisdom, and he was loved by God and by all who knew him.

—Luke 2:51-52 NLT

The husband was talking to a good friend on the phone when his wife was trying to get his attention.

"Yeah, wasn't that great? I busted a gut laughing at that one . . ."

"Honey," she whispered, seemingly to no one.

"And can you believe what Frank said? Man, if I had been that guy . . ."

"Honey," she tried again.

"No way, no how. Next time, I'm afraid he won't be so lucky . . ."

"Honey . . . Honey! I need to talk to you."

"Just . . . just a minute, John." "Yes, Julie, I'm talking to John, what do you want? What is it?" "No, no. I'm still here, John . . . No, I don't have to hang up . . . Just a second . . ." "Hey, Julie, can't you see I'm busy? What's so important?"

It isn't always easy to live out your faith at home. It can be easy to talk about your faith outside the home or with a group of nice people at church, but when you actually have to take action—when you are forced to stop thinking only about yourself and are challenged to do something for others day in and day out, things become a little more difficult. This is true especially at home. Whether it's your children, your spouse, your parents, or your roommate—any of the people with whom you share a home—these are people who know you, people who know your strengths and weaknesses, your good points and bad, what makes you tick, and the hundred different ways to get under your skin. These are people who are not easily fooled and who know what kind of life you live behind closed doors. They are the first to know if your faith talk matches your faith walk.

Even Jesus lived out his faith at home. Being the son of God, he didn't necessarily have to do so. After all, who would have a better excuse to ignore parental guidance and set himself apart from his family than Jesus, especially if he was doing his heavenly Father's work? But Jesus chose to live out his faith at home by being obedient to his parents: "Then he returned to Nazareth with them and was obedient to them" (Luke 2:51 NLT).

How can you live out your faith at home? You can start by being obedient—obedient to your position as a spouse, a parent, or a caring friend. Be respectful of others, whether it is in regard to their time, their possessions, or their unique personality. Look for ways to serve others. Find ways to encourage the persons in your household. Keep in mind that your journey of faith might be very different from the faith journey of someone else in your family. Look for the good in others as though your life depended on it—because it does. There is nothing more lonely than the solitary life of a person who cares only for himself or herself. And remember that we love others because God first loved us.

God calls us to live out our faith at home day-by-day, minute-by-minute, task-by-task. This may not be easy, and it almost assuredly will not be glamorous, but it will help you discover how God wants you to serve him as you, too, begin to grow in wisdom.

PRAYER

Dear God, help me live out my faith at home through my actions. Help me be obedient in fulfilling the many roles you have given me. Help me grow in your love and wisdom. Amen.

FOCUS FOR THE DAY

Today I will start to live out my faith at home.

PERSONAL REFLECTION TIME

What does it mean for you to live out your faith at home? Do you think it is more important to live out your faith at home or when you are away from home? Explain. Do you find it easier to live out your faith at home or away from home? Explain. What actions can you start doing today—this minute—that will better enable you to live out your faith at home?

Day Two   **With Relatives**

For we are God's workmanship, created in Christ Jesus to do good works, which God prepared in advance for us to do.
                                            —Ephesians 2:10 NIV

As a member of the family of God, you already have more relatives than you can count. You are a member of a worldwide family of Christians from all walks of life. Through Christ you are related to famous people as well as unknowns. You have fellow believers in most every nation, every city, every town, and most every village. And you all have at least one thing in common—a commitment to God through Jesus Christ.

Family is important to God. Just look at the long lists of genealogy in the early books of the Bible. It's not just the names of mothers, fathers, sons, and daughters that are listed. There are also aunts, uncles, cousins, and nephews listed by name. This shows how every person has a place and a role in the Kingdom. God loves and includes everyone, without exception. And God wants us to be connected.

We are already connected to some family members. You may see them at weddings or funerals. Some you may keep in touch with. They are aunts or uncles, cousins or nephews, and in-laws who drop by occasionally. Perhaps you send them Christmas cards or exchange gifts. God loves them all, as much as God loves you. And God has connected all of you for a purpose.

Relatives, those distant as well as close, are different from strangers in several ways. You may know them by name; perhaps you share some common interests, and you are connected by blood. To different degrees, you have a relationship with those you call relatives. And because you have a relationship, you can touch their lives because you are close to them. Ministry to others begins with familiarity.

Whether you realize it or not, you are already a witness to family. Your behavior at family gatherings is a witness to your faith as is your language. You know how words and actions go together. Just as you have observed your relatives for years, they have also been observing your words and deeds. What have they been seeing?

You can find out what others see in you by becoming closer. The connection God wants you to have with others can be strengthened by just getting together. If your cousin, for example, does not have a church home, extend an invitation to attend just with you. If a relative needs help, minister to them. If you need help, ask a relative. In mutual need, the bonds of family grow stronger. You get better connected. And you never know where a conversation might lead when God is concerned.

Keep love in the family by becoming better connected to your relatives. Love them as you love yourself. That's what God wants. God has brought these people into your life for a purpose. It's no accident. As you continue your devotions, remember them in prayer. Support them spiritually. Bless your relatives and allow them to bless you.

As Ralph Waldo Emerson once observed, "The glory of friendship is not the outstretched hand, nor the kindly smile, nor the joy of companionship; it's the spiritual inspiration that comes to one when he discovers that someone believes in him and is willing to trust him with his friendship."

Be daring. Befriend a relative. It's a way of keeping love in the family.

PRAYER

Dear God, thank you for all of my relatives. Help me to realize we are all connected. Remind me of the importance of family. Show me the joy of getting to know people better. And help me put my good intentions into action. Amen.

FOCUS FOR THE DAY

Today I will connect with at least one relative, by a phone call, letter, or e-mail.

PERSONAL REFLECTION TIME

Reflect upon all of your relatives. List them by name. Picture them in your mind. Think about how you can become better connected with them. What opportunities do you have to help a family member in the name of Jesus?

Day Three   **In Your Neighborhood**

On one occasion an expert in the law stood up to test Jesus. "Teacher," he asked, "what must I do to inherit eternal life?" "What is written in the Law?" he replied. "How do you read it?" He answered: " 'Love the Lord your God with all your heart and with all your soul and with all your strength and with all your mind'; and, 'Love your neighbor as yourself.' " "You have answered correctly," Jesus replied. "Do this and you will live." But he wanted to justify himself, so he asked Jesus, "And who is my neighbor?"
                                             —Luke 10:25-29 NIV

It is a troubled neighborhood. You don't want to go outdoors after dark. It's a dangerous place out there. Gangs rule the streets and fight among themselves. Drugs and sex are for sale on certain street corners. Drive-by shootings occur on a regular basis. Five people have been murdered within the past year.

It is a real neighborhood, perhaps one of dozens scattered across inner cities in the United States. If you live in a metropolitan area, you know where it is, and you steer clear of it, unless you live there. But good people live there. They do their best to survive, and they are working together to make their neighborhood better. To take back the neighborhood is their goal. And every time a resident dies a violent death, neighbors hold a peace vigil at the crime scene. Flowers and teddy bears holding hearts sit at a doorstep in memory of a lost life. It's not a beautiful day in that neighborhood.

Everyone wants to live in a good neighborhood. Whether you live in rural Iowa or in a metropolitan inner city, quality of life matters. We all struggle with more or less the same neighborhood issues. And, in reality, we are all neighbors.

When Jesus was asked, "And who is my neighbor?" he responded with the parable of the good Samaritan. The neighbor, it turns out, is anyone in need. It's a person who needs help. The parable encourages people to go out of their way to minister to others. Exceed expectations; be a servant, asking nothing in return. That's what you call a good Samaritan.

Neighbors and neighborhoods both need good Samaritans. Today we might call them good neighbors. It's easy to be one. You look out for each other. You know the names of people on your block. You call police when you spot suspicious activity. In two words, you are an *active participant* in your corner of the world. You are involved because you are a servant of Jesus Christ.

That's what God seeks from us—involvement. Doing the right thing. Connecting with others whether or not it is convenient. Being part of the solution to neighborhood problems. Modeling Christian behavior at neighborhood gatherings. Taking good care of your property. Putting your faith to work right where you live. And maybe it's time to redefine the borders of your neighborhood to include areas where you don't want to be after dark.

Who is my neighbor? You know the answer. Perhaps a better question is, how can I help my neighbor? Good neighbors and good neighborhoods are contagious. Begin where you live. Be a blessing to your neighborhood.

PRAYER

Dear God, thank you for placing me in this neighborhood. I want my neighbors to see a person who reflects the love of Jesus when they look at me. Guide my words and actions to be pleasing to you and to my neighbors. Help me be your servant in a neighborhood without boundaries. Amen.

FOCUS FOR THE DAY

Today I will be a good neighbor by opening my eyes and ears to the needs of others.

PERSONAL REFLECTION TIME

Reflect upon the needs of your neighbors and the neighborhood. Think about how you can live out your faith by taking a greater role in making your neighborhood a better place to live.

Day Four   **In the Community**

I pray that Christ Jesus and the church will forever bring praise to God. His power at work in us can do far more than we dare ask or imagine.

—Ephesians 3:20-21 CEV

A favorite question teenagers like to ask in Bible school is, "If God is the all-powerful Creator, can he make a rock so big that even he can't lift it?"

The problem with most people's faith is not that God isn't big enough, rather it is the limits they put on God in terms of how God works in the world. We simply do not have a big-enough God; we tend to think of God in terms of limits. Rather than letting God work as God wants, people put up gates, restrictions, before God can begin. They see a problem or a barrier cross in their path, and instead of asking God to remove it, they simply don't believe it can be removed. They stop God's work before it starts. They limit how God is able to act in their lives.

Think about it. What limits have you placed on God? When was the last time you prayed expecting God to work out an impossible situation? In a broken relationship do you expect God to work miracles, or do you assume that you have done what you can and that there is nothing more to be done? In terms of world peace, do you just assume the world will be at war forever, or do you pray and believe daily that despite all the evidence to the contrary, God will find ways to create peace one person at a time? Have you given in to health challenges and resigned yourself to a grim diagnosis? Or have you given God the room to work so that the impossible might happen? Are there people in your community who need to see God's love in action but do not because others have placed their own limits on how God might act, or on who deserves the love of God?

When Paul wrote his letter to the Ephesians, he was writing to people who had been putting limits on God. They didn't think Jews and Gentiles could get along in peace, especially in terms of faith. But Paul didn't put the same limits on God. He wrote, "Christ has made peace between Jews and Gentiles, and he has united us by breaking down the wall of hatred that separated us. . . . He even brought Jews and Gentiles together as though we were only one person, when he united us in peace" (Ephesians 2:14-15 CEV).

Where is there hatred in your community? Where have walls been built that keep people from loving one another? Look there, and you will see an opportunity for God to act.

What has God challenged you to do in terms of your community? How might you spread acceptance and peace and respect to those not in your faith community? How can you work with your local government and church officials to meet people's basic needs of food, clothing, and shelter, not to mention respect and love? If you think one person can't make a difference, think of Mother Teresa. Think of Billy Graham. Think of Martin Luther King Jr. and countless others. They believed in what God could accomplish, and then they got out of the way and let God work. As Paul reminds us, God's "power at work in us can do far more than we dare ask or imagine" (Ephesians 3:21 CEV).

PRAYER

Dear God, take away the many ways in which I limit your work in my life. Help me be your instrument for change in my community. Amen.

FOCUS FOR THE DAY

Today I will not put limits on how God is able to work in my community.

PERSONAL REFLECTION TIME

In what ways have you put limits on God in the past? Have there been times when you simply thought it was beyond God's power to act? Have there been times when God has surprised you with doing far more than you had asked or imagined? Explain. How can you give God more room to act in your own community?

Day Five   **At Work**

Just as our bodies have many parts and each part has a special function, so it is with Christ's body. We are all parts of his one body, and each of us has different work to do. And since we are all one body in Christ, we belong to each other, and each of us needs all the others.

—Romans 12:4-5 NLT

The visitor walked into the lobby of a large office building and asked, "How many people work here?"

"Oh, about one in every ten!" responded the employer.

It's not always easy to put our hearts and souls into our jobs. In Paul's letter to the Ephesians, he deals with two aspects of the work we do. First, he addresses work in terms of *what we do*—how we use the skills and talents God has given us in our daily lives. Second, Paul addresses our work in terms of *who we are;* even at work, we are people of God.

Regarding *what we do*, Paul writes, "Just as our bodies have many parts and each part has a special function, so it is with Christ's body. We are all parts of his one body, and each of us has different work to do." Paul recognizes that we are not all equally gifted in the same areas; there are many parts and different functions within the body of Christ.

What do you do well? What do you like to do? Do you like working with people? Do you love digging into details? Would you rather work on your own or with others? Do other people energize you or drain you? Do you have a gift for teaching? for leading others? Do you like working with your hands? Do you enjoy plants or animals?

God has given you a unique personality with unique gifts.

Although some people advocate working in an area you absolutely love, the reality is that what we love to do may not always provide us with the income we need. The things we love to do may turn out instead to be our hobby. But Paul's challenge to us in the text is to understand our uniqueness and to use our gifts for the betterment of others, whether that means picking up trash or performing brain surgery.

Regarding *who we are*, Paul writes, "Since we are all one body in Christ, we belong to each other, and each of us needs all the others." We do not live or work as lone individuals—what we do influences those around us at home and at work. It is not "us against them" or Christians versus non-Christians when we go to work. We are not to ignore people who may be unbelievers, but rather we are to witness by our actions and live with them in a spirit of peace. The people in Ephesus had divided people into two groups, the Jews and the Gentiles (non-Jews). The Jews were God's chosen people, it was said by some, while the Gentiles were not. Paul's letter affirms that both are part of God's family.

When we are at work, our role is to be ambassadors for Christ. Our work is a place to live out who we are as people of faith—people who are able to love, accept, respect, and forgive others.

God's purpose remains the same whether we are at work or at home: to save people, whether they are Jew or Gentile, residents or strangers, good or bad, plumber or doctor, lawyer or assembly worker. The places we work give us the unique challenge to live out our faith not only by what we do but by who we are, and through how we treat others as part of the body of Christ.

PRAYER

Lord, no matter where I work, help me serve you as I use my gifts. Thank you for all of the unique people you have created to work together to accomplish your purposes. Amen.

FOCUS FOR THE DAY

Today I will serve God in what I do at work and in how I treat the people with whom I work.

PERSONAL REFLECTION TIME

What has been your favorite/least favorite job or place to work? Why did you enjoy/not enjoy working there: was it because of the type of work you did, or was it because of the people with whom you worked? Explain. Do people judge you at work—in a positive, negative, or indifferent way—because of your faith? In terms of living out your faith, what special challenges do you face at work? Explain.

Day Six   At Church

Behold, I will do a new thing; now it shall spring forth; shall ye not know it? I will even make a way in the wilderness, and rivers in the desert.

Isaiah 43:19 KJV

This book began with an idea—actually, over 200 of them. Back in the early 1990s, the authors of this book compiled ideas for church leaders, and *The Church Idea Book* was published by Abingdon Press. That book led to others, and now it has led to this one, but it all started with the concept that ideas, especially church ideas, need to be shared.

That in itself is a powerful idea. We all have ideas, you know. They pop into our minds off and on during the week as invited or uninvited visitors. For example, we get the idea that we can do something better, or we think to ourselves that a situation needs a specific solution. Much of the time our ideas amount to nothing. Like good intentions, they remain good ideas until they vanish from our minds.

But once in a while, ideas become reality. That's exciting, especially when they happen within the church. The church needs new ideas to proclaim the gospel in new and different ways. Too often we stick with what's familiar, or variations of it. There is a comfort level for us in the familiar and the safe. For example, when it comes to the worship service, many of us like the same hymns, the same order of service, and the same events year after year. And there is nothing wrong with that. Doing things the same way usually upsets no one. There is not much of an outcry for change. But there should be.

For one, our faith needs to change in order to grow. Perhaps that is why you are reading this book. You are ready for a closer relationship with Jesus Christ. This means you want to put your faith into action.

There is no better place to grow your faith than in the church. The church is where people come together for exactly the same reasons—to worship God, to have Christian fellowship together, and to further their spiritual development. This begins with ideas—and the courage to change.

There are few better ways to touch lives than by sharing your faith within your local congregation. It might be through teaching a Sunday school class or by participating in a weekly Bible study. Maybe the Lord needs you on the church council. Somewhere there is a job waiting for you. Open your eyes and ears. Every church has a need for active members who can get things done. Too often only a handful of people do the majority of the ministry within a church.

It isn't always easy. It means showing up at church more often than just on Sunday mornings. It means taking the time to meet new people and develop new relationships. That can be scary and time-consuming. It means contributing fresh ideas to old problems, even though your ideas might not be accepted. Taking risks is a necessary action step for living out your faith, inside and outside of the church.

Perhaps you are God's idea of what your church needs. Talk to God about it. Maybe the time has come for your voice to be heard. Think about it. It's just an idea.

PRAYER

Dear God, the church is your home, and it is also my home. Help me to make it a place of love and peace. Grant that it may be a welcoming and accepting home for those who seek a closer relationship with Jesus. Thank you for allowing me to be a part of this life-changing congregation. Show me how I can help. Amen.

FOCUS FOR THE DAY

Today I will be open to new ideas and see new possibilities for faith in action.

PERSONAL REFLECTION TIME

Reflect on your involvement in the church. Think about how your church can become more effective in ministry. Consider your skills and how you can combine your faith and ideas to be part of the solution to the challenges faced by your church.

Day Seven   **In the World**

"All things are possible with God."
—Mark 10:27 NIV

Where in the world do you begin to change the world? That is today's question, and the answer centers on whether or not you believe your faith can have an impact far from home. Our troubled planet certainly needs help, but what can one person do?

The odds are against you. You are fighting against poverty, malnutrition, AIDS, war, terrorism, racism, corrupted governments, dictatorships, nuclear weapons, and increasing division between the haves and the have-nots of our world. While even prosperous nations like the United States struggle to meet the needs of their citizens, the poorest of the poor nations often struggle without much hope. For many nations, the future is bleak.

So where do you start? How can you begin to resolve problems and situations that have existed throughout history? And if governments with many resources can't fix things, how can individuals? Again you may ask, *Can one person make a difference?*

Yes. Individuals throughout history have been instruments of change. Consider the people who have worked together to develop new medicines that save and prolong lives. Inventors have changed the face of communication and technology. Leaders of some nations have worked for peaceful solutions to global problems. The quality of health care is slowly improving. Better education is helping to gradually raise the standard of living in many nations. Yet there is so much more to be done.

Although the problems seem overwhelming, that isn't stopping committed individuals who are trying to be part of the solution. Some teachers are traveling to foreign lands to promote literacy. Doctors are leaving American cities and going to the poorest areas of the world to provide medical care. Churches are sending congregational members to build houses and deliver other necessities in places where they are truly needed. Farmers are leaving their farms to teach agricultural techniques to people who live across the ocean. They are all trying to make a difference.

How can you help? You can offer your support by becoming an active participant in organizations that want to solve world problems. You can set aside some of your money as a donation to help pay for projects in areas of need. You can vote for candidates for political office who have a global viewpoint. And you can search the Internet and do research in your local library to discover new opportunities for getting involved. We are all connected.

In order to change the world, good intentions must be accompanied by individual acts of faith. You must believe that by working with others, we can make the world a better place. There is still time to save lives and repair broken dreams. Jesus needs his followers to be global good Samaritans.

Where do you start? Begin where you can, and do what you can do. Any effort will help. Use your creativity, and team up with others. Provide hope, help, and healing. God created you, and God empowers you to make a world of difference.

PRAYER

Dear God, the world is a mess, and it seems to be getting worse. Make me an agent of change and part of the solution to global problems. I want the people of the world to have food, water, and a roof over their heads, and a good quality of life. Show me how I can make a difference. Help me move beyond good intentions and perform acts of faith. Amen.

FOCUS FOR THE DAY

Today I will have a global outlook, and I will think and pray about ways in which God is calling me to be a responsible world citizen.

PERSONAL REFLECTION TIME

Reflect on the skills and resources you possess that can benefit others who are in need. Consider how all the people of the world are connected. Plan to act in faith on behalf of Jesus.

How Are Things Going?
Week Five

For instructions on using the chart below, see page 31.

		Sun	Mon	Tues	Wed	Thurs	Fri	Sat
Daily Devotion	Date							
	Scripture							
	Devotion							
	Prayer							
	Focus for the Day							
	Reflection Time							
Daily Prayers	Morning							
	Meals							
	Bedtime							
	Other							

WEEK SIX
Go with God

Introduction

As you enter the final week of this part of your spiritual journey, you may be wondering about the future. After you have completed this book, what is next? Don't worry about it.

That's the essence of what Henry Ward Beecher meant when he wrote, "No matter what looms ahead, if you can eat today, enjoy the sunlight today, mix good cheer with friends today, enjoy it and bless God for it. Do not look back on happiness—or dream of it in the future. You are only sure of today; do not let yourself be cheated out of it."

Beecher was a wise man. He knew that you can do nothing about the past, and you can't control the future. The present moment is your only certainty. And it is another gift from God.

God wants you to make the most of today and to leave the future to him. Things have a way of working out where God is concerned. Over the past five weeks, you have witnessed the power of God in action. Together you and God have covered a lot of territory. You've discovered the blessings of spending time together, overcome roadblocks, learned the value of listening, put your faith into action, and lived out your faith in the world. Now, the best is yet to come.

There is an old saying for people going on a journey: "Go with God." It is a blessing and a prayer. It reminds the traveler that God is with them and will protect them, and that God will provide for their needs along the way. This week signals a beginning, not an ending. You will be exploring new possibilities for ministry through readings and reflection. Over the next week, a new series of spiritual adventures will start. God will continue to amaze and challenge you. Treasure each day and every moment of life. Do your best. That's all that God asks.

Go with God. Your future is in God's hands. And that's the safest place to be.

Day One   **Good Works**

> *The desire of the righteous ends only in good,*
> *but the hope of the wicked only in wrath.*
> *One man gives freely, yet gains even more;*
> *another withholds unduly, but comes to poverty.*
> *A generous man will prosper;*
> *he who refreshes others will himself be refreshed.*
> —Proverbs 11:23-25 NIV

You've just begun your sixth week of spending regular daily time with God. If you are like most people, you have had some struggles along the way, a few questions, and many rewards. And you have probably thought to yourself at one time or another, *Is it really worth it? Is it worth it to keep my focus, my energy, and my time on God, even if nothing seems to be happening? Is it worth it to stay in the fight?*

A sign in the aisle of Wal-Mart reads, "Doing the good things good neighbors do. And we believe good works." There's a larger sign hanging near the ceiling, big enough to let you know that the message it carries is serious. The sign, six feet long and two feet high, simply reads: "Good works." Underneath this motto is listed the Wal-Mart corporate philosophy and values.

Doing good; it works. Good really works. We didn't need Wal-Mart to tell us that—it's not an original idea, after all—but still it is a helpful reminder as we live out our faith in a world that does not always seem to reward good. We get the same reminder from the book of Proverbs (11:23-25), as though the writer is saying, "Stay in the game, fight the good fight, keep doing good, because it works." Or in the writer's own words, "The desire of the righteous ends only in good." Do the right thing. Stay focused on God. Stay focused on others. Good works.

The apostle Paul said the same thing from his jail cell shortly before his death. "I have fought the good fight, I have finished the race, I have kept the faith. Now there is in store for me the crown of righteousness, which the Lord, the righteous Judge, will award to me on that day—and not only to me, but also to all who have longed for his appearing" (2 Timothy 4:7-8 NIV). But we do not have to wait until death to see God's rewards. Our faith is not simply pie in the sky, a hopeful wish that may or may not come true after we depart this world. God works in the world. God works through us. Even if it's in some small way, lives have changed, people have been saved, hope has been restored, the sick have been healed, the lonely have been visited, and you have come to know God more intimately. Good works.

Yes, good works. And so does God. In fact, this is the reason the writer in Proverbs knows beyond a shadow of a doubt that the righteous and the generous will be rewarded. He has seen God work firsthand. He has seen God alive in the world, bringing order out of chaos and meaning out of meaninglessness. Good works; our faith is not in vain; we will be rewarded because God is working through us. That is our hope. That is our promise.

As we continue to discover God and let God loose in our lives, we will do the good God wants us to do. Not because of our own good, but because of our God. Good works. And so does God.

PRAYER

Dear God, give me the strength and courage and faith to continue seeking you. Remind me that living for you is not in vain, but that *doing good* works because of you. Amen.

Focus for the Day

Today I will remember that *doing good* works, because God works.

Personal Reflection Time

In what ways have you seen God work in your own life? How have you been changed? How has God worked through others to reach you with healing or comfort or peace or strength? Would you agree that doing good works? Why or why not?

Day Two   **The Place of Prayer**

> *Pray without ceasing.*
> —1 Thessalonians 5:17 KJV

There's a saying that if you are too busy to pray, you are too busy.

Too often we think that spending time with God happens only in certain settings or at certain times: in church; while reading the Bible; in the quiet of our home. But in his letter to the Thessalonians, Paul encourages them to "pray without ceasing."

Instead of limiting God to a certain time or place or setting, why not expand your idea of the ways in which God can work? Use the world and your "spare" moments as an opportunity to pray. The following are just a few ways you might begin to do this.

While watching the news on TV. The daily or nightly news is chock-full of things you can pray for. When a certain event moves you, simply ask for God's help for that situation. For example, for a war being waged halfway across the world, you can simply pray, "Lord, bring peace to that area." For a family that has experienced hardship, you can quickly say, "Bring healing in whatever way is needed, Lord." Certain events may make you think of something going on in your own life or in the life of someone you know. A report on cancer research may remind you of a friend recently diagnosed with cancer, and so you pray, "Dear God, thanks for bringing healing and peace to Linda." You can do the same thing when listening to the news on the radio in your car. (Just don't close your eyes when praying in the car—driving blindly is certainly not necessary for God to hear you!)

On the way to work. Use "stopping times" as times to stop and pray. At the stop sign, at the stoplight, when stopped because of traffic delays or construction work—use this time to remember those who need your prayers. It can be just one or two words, a name, or just the reason for praying: "This morning's meeting." "Sharon." "Depression." Again, God will know what the specific need is.

In a "flash." These are also quick prayers, offered on the spur of the moment because of something you see. You're on the bus and see someone on the sidewalk that seems to need help: "Help him, Lord." You're in the checkout line at the grocery store and spot someone who could use a prayer: "Help meet her needs, Lord." You're filling up your car with gas and notice a couple arguing in the car next to you: "Love them, Lord." While you're on the treadmill at the gym, you suddenly remember something you said to someone else that you now regret: "Forgive me, Lord."

Unlike the pagan gods in the apostle Paul's time, our God is not limited to a shrine, or a particular place, or a ritual, or any certain time, or perfect circumstances. God is always available to us. There is no inappropriate time or place to pray to our Lord. God works in our world, day in and day out, and in the midst of the good and the bad. That is our place of prayer.

Dear Lord, remind me that you are always more ready to listen than I am to pray. Thank you for being available whenever I need you. Amen.

FOCUS FOR THE DAY

Today I will try to pray without ceasing, knowing that God is always listening to me.

PERSONAL REFLECTION TIME

"If you are too busy to pray, then you are too busy"; do you agree or disagree, and why? Using the examples in the devotion above as thought-starters, think of times throughout the day when you can offer a quick prayer to God.

Day Three   **Praise the Lord**

> *Praise the LORD, I tell myself;*
> * with my whole heart, I will praise his holy name.*
> *Praise the LORD, I tell myself,*
> * and never forget the good things he does for me.*
> *He forgives all my sins*
> * and heals all my diseases.*
> *He ransoms me from death*
> * and surrounds me with love and tender mercies.*
> *He fills my life with good things.*
> * My youth is renewed like the eagle's!*
> *   —Psalm 103:1-5 NLT*

The prisoner sat in solitary confinement, alone, dejected. He was sitting still now, though his thoughts seemed to bounce around from wall to wall. This was a reflection of what was going on inside his head—thoughts that would not keep still. His life was a mess. What was it he had heard on the radio? To praise God in every situation? To praise God his whole life, whether he felt like it or not, whether he had reason to or not, whether he thought it would help or not?

So he began to praise God—slowly, uncertainly. "Praise the Lord for being in prison . . . Praise the Lord for being in solitary confinement . . . Praise the Lord for the darkness . . . Praise the Lord for this terrible food . . . Praise the Lord . . ." And slowly, bit by bit, his attitude changed—and then his life. He is out of prison now, helping other prisoners change their es for the better. According to him, it all began in that small, dark prison cell with a word of praise.

Obviously the psalmist was onto something.

Praise the LORD, I tell myself;
　with my whole heart, I will praise his holy name.
Praise the LORD, I tell myself,
　and never forget the good things he does for me." (verses 1-2 NLT)

Praise works because it takes our focus off ourselves and places it on God. It redirects our self-pity and places our problems into the hands of God—someone who can do something about it. Rather than being self-directed, praise is God directed. And who better to focus our attention on than God, the One who "forgives all my sins / and heals all my diseases. / He ransoms me from death / and surrounds me with love and tender mercies. / He fills my life with good things" (verses 3-5 NLT).

Praise the Lord. Unfortunately, this can often be used as an empty, catchall phrase with little true meaning. But as the psalmist and the prisoner both discovered, it is a power-packed formula for giving your situation, and your life, over to the God of the universe, the God who gives us life and all good things. *Praise the Lord.* Three simple words give hope and life and salvation.

Praise the Lord. Praise the Lord. Praise the Lord. Give it a try, and see if it doesn't change your life as well.

PRAYER

Dear Lord, help me praise you in all things. You give me all that I have and all that I need. Amen.

FOCUS FOR THE DAY

Today I will praise the Lord.

PERSONAL REFLECTION TIME

Do you think it's possible for such a simple phrase like "Praise the Lord" to change a person's life? Why or why not? Has there been a time in your own life when giving thanks or praise made a difference? Explain. What things can you praise the Lord for right now? Friends? Family? Shelter? Health?

Day Four   **Expect the Unexpected**

When an honest person wins, it's time to celebrate; / when crooks are in control, it's best to hide.
—Proverbs 28:12 CEV

The man was on foot chasing after a thief who was riding away with his bicycle. It was a new bike, and an expensive one at that, and he didn't want to lose it. But this man quickly learned, you can't win a footrace against a young bicyclist. That's when John came to his rescue.

John witnessed what had happened, pulled up in his car to the frustrated victim, and suddenly the odds had changed. It was now car against bike. Together, the two men chased the bicycle thief for blocks and blocks. The bicyclist kept going as fast as he could in an attempt to escape from the neighborhood. After a while, it looked like the thief might still win. How could he be stopped? Something needed to happen.

And it did. Another motorist had also witnessed the theft and was also giving chase, although no one knew it. At a busy intersection, the second motorist pulled her car in front of the escaping bicyclist and knocked him off the bike. All traffic suddenly stopped to watch what was happening before their eyes. To them it looked like an accident. As John and the bike's owner arrived on the scene, they witnessed the stunned thief picking himself up off the concrete street and limping off in an attempt to flee. He vanished between some nearby houses.

Everyone was shaken by what had occurred. John said that he was glad someone else intervened. He admitted he had no plan of action to stop the thief. John simply had seen an injustice and just wanted to help.

What would you have done in this situation? What would Jesus have done? If John had not become involved, would there have been a different result? There are any number of outcomes that could have taken place. The thief easily could have escaped with the bike, or he could have been badly injured or killed. A bystander remarked that the guy might think twice before he ever tried to steal a bike again.

This story is not a parable, but a true-life situation in a real world. Yet there are lessons to be learned from it. "Thou shalt not steal" certainly comes to mind. Also, that it is good to come to the aid of a person in need (although it must be said that giving chase to a thief yourself usually is not recommended). All parties involved were risk-takers. And one person had a plan of action while the other did not. This time good won over evil. That isn't always the case.

Life is a teacher. And one of life's best teachers is experience. That is one of the reasons God put you here.

Unexpected situations test your ability to respond. You never know when you will be tested. Life can be a pop quiz. You are given choices. Situations have many possible resolutions. You learn by doing, and you learn from your mistakes. And you try not to make the same mistake twice.

Oliver Wendell Holmes observed, "To reach the port of heaven, we must sail sometimes with the wind and sometimes against it—but we must sail, and not drift, nor lie at anchor."

Get involved in life today. You can make a difference. And get ready for your next lesson in life. It's part of God's plan to keep you on your toes.

PRAYER

Dear God, thank you for life's exciting moments. I often have a mixture of fear and anticipation of what will happen next. Remind me that through Jesus I can handle anything that comes my way. I will do my best to be your servant. Amen.

FOCUS FOR THE DAY

Today I will be ready for whatever God sends my way.

PERSONAL REFLECTION TIME

Reflect on some of life's adventures that God has sent your way. What lessons have you learned by being an active participant in life?

Day Five   **Let God Be God**

And my God will meet all your needs according to his glorious riches in Christ Jesus.

—Philippians 4:19 NIV

During the Great Depression, a group of farmers assembled in a church in drought-stricken Kansas to pray for badly needed rain. As the preacher stood before the farmers, he looked over the group and asked the question, "Where are your umbrellas?"

That's the way many people treat their faith and the power of prayer. They believe in a God who is able to do anything, but their expectations fall short when it comes to results. There seems to be a gap between faith in theory and faith in practice. It's a mixed message. We pray for a shower of blessings, yet deep inside we expect the drought to continue.

What's the problem? Maybe it's because of unanswered prayer. The fact is, we don't get everything we ask for—and that can be discouraging. For many people, praying is like hoping for luck—we feel like the odds are against us, but we try anyway. Maybe this time we'll hit it big. Maybe this time God will be on our side. Maybe this time God will grant our request.

The trouble is, we often fail to realize what we are asking, why we are asking it, and that we are asking for *our* will to be done, rather than *God's* will. God is not the problem; it's us. Often we ask for things that would harm us. Or we ask for what we do not really need. God's answer may be to wait, or it may be a flat-out no, and that is really hard for us to accept.

Perhaps God is trying to teach us something, and being the humans we are, we tend to be slow learners. God's lesson for us may be that you don't always get what you want. Imagine if every prayer request was granted! Think of the disasters! Another lesson may be that there is good and evil in the world, and good isn't always the victor. God will triumph in the end, but our daily struggles may not end with the results we want. God is with us, and God loves us, but our loving Father clearly sees the big picture. Father knows best. Our vision and knowledge are simply limited.

Let God be God. That's what is important. God has the

power and uses it with our best interests in mind. God wants us to pray, God wants us to be persistent, but we have to respect God's will. That's the bottom line.

God's intentions are divine intentions. Our intentions are merely good. That makes a world of difference when it comes to our prayer life. But keep praying. Eventually there will be a downpour. And then you'll want to have your umbrella handy.

PRAYER

Dear God, thank you for not always giving me what I ask for in prayer. Help me realize that you know best. Give me the wisdom to match my requests with your will. Help me listen to your voice. May my prayers reflect spiritual maturity and be pleasing to you. Amen.

FOCUS FOR THE DAY

Today I will respect the power of prayer and be open to unexpected answers.

PERSONAL REFLECTION TIME

Reflect on your questions about prayer. Think about your prayer history. Consider your past requests and how God has answered you. How can you have a more effective prayer life in the future? What should prayer also be about besides just making requests?

Day Six   Life Isn't Fair. God Is.

"No one has greater love than this, to lay down one's life for one's friends."

—John 15:13 NRSV

If you were listening to the local news at all, it was hard to miss. The news media in Minneapolis-St. Paul, over a period of weeks, covered the stories of three good Samaritans who died while trying to help persons in need. It was enough to make some think twice about performing random acts of kindness.

The first good Samaritan, a man, had stopped on a busy freeway to help a woman with a flat tire. A car plowed into them, trapping the man under the car. Passing motorists then became good Samaritans themselves and lifted the car off the injured man. He died days later. In another incident, a man stopped to help a woman who had hit a deer with her car. The man died after being struck by a car while crossing the free-way in the fog. And then there was the clerk at a gas station who attempted to stop a teenage bully from harassing a devel-opmentally challenged customer. The bully left the gas sta-tion, returned with a gun, and shot the clerk to death.

Living is risky business. You never know what's going to happen in the next minute, hour, or day. It seems that death often is lurking, ready to take advantage of any mis-take or to join forces with evil to destroy a life or two. No one is immune to danger. The randomness scares the life out of us at times. Isn't God supposed to be in control?

The question of why bad things happen to good people has baffled people for centuries. Some might respond that it is the will of God. That's an easy answer, but is it the right one? Surely many things happen in this world that are not God's will. The loss of nearly three thousand lives in the World Trade Center attack was not a part of God's plan. Yet God allowed it to happen. Evil triumphed over good. And again you ask, Why?

We live in an imperfect world. That's one of the causes. The bad things that happen to good people are symptoms of these imperfections. People don't drive the way they should, and there are accidents. Guns are readily available. Drugs and alcohol cloud people's minds and judgment.

Human beings mess up. And because of these reasons and others, sometimes things go terribly wrong.

This is not how God intended life to be. Long ago, sin entered into the world, and things haven't been the same since. Yet God is in control. God's will shall be done on earth as it is in heaven. It is God who often has to clean up our messes and who salvages good from evil. Untimely deaths are not God's choice, nor are they ours, but they are a fact of life. Love heals some of the damage, and we believe that good will win out over evil; however, often that still leaves us in a world of hurt.

Perhaps what really matters is how we live, and what we do with the time we have. We can control that. A strong relationship with Christ empowers us to handle the risks of life. We can be good Samaritans despite the costs. The values of love, truth, honesty, patience, kindness, charity, and forgiveness are enough to help us over life's rough spots. The world is unfair, but God is both fair and faithful.

Good Samaritans have nothing to fear. The Bible tells us that nothing can snatch us out of God's hand. Jesus defeated death, and some day, evil too will be defeated. Until then, we are servants of the Lord in a crazy world that's our temporary home.

PRAYER

Dear God, this world seems so dangerous at times. I wonder what will happen next. Help me not to fear, but to focus on you. Help me to take risks, and to be your hands and voice to those in need. I know that you love me and are always with me. That's all I need to know. Amen.

FOCUS FOR THE DAY

Today I will do the work the Lord asks of me, regardless of risks. I am a servant of Jesus Christ.

Reflect on what you can do to make the world a better place. Think about how you can put your faith into action.

Day Seven   Go with God

"Lord, now lettest thou thy servant depart in peace, according to thy word:/ For mine eyes have seen thy salvation."
—Luke 2:29-30 KJV

Where do I go from here? That's a question we all ask ourselves at one time or another. Whether a journey is about to begin or about to end, we want to know what direction to take next. There is a sense of security when you map out your next destination. And it's just plain smart to have a travel plan in life.

As this is the last day of this particular spiritual adventure, perhaps you are asking that very question. *What's my destination now?* You have been walking with the Lord each day for six weeks, and now you face a fork in the road. Like a college student leaving home for the first time, you have some decisions to make. What do you pack for this next journey?

The answer is different for each person, but here are some suggestions:

Take along your relationship with Jesus Christ. Continue your spiritual growth. Talk to God every day. Ask for guidance and faith for the journey.

Pack your prayer book and your Bible. They are sources of wisdom, inspiration, and direction. They will keep you from getting lost in the world.

Include a new book of daily meditations or devotions. Visit a Christian bookstore or your church library. Devotions make excellent spiritual road maps.

Carry a commitment to be a servant of Jesus Christ wherever you go. Serve those in need. Perform random acts of kindness. Be a voice for change and a voice of compassion.

Stop in at church on a regular basis. You can get spiritual fuel for your journey there. Take advantage of opportunities for education and fellowship. You don't have to be alone. And besides, it's more fun to travel with others.

And finally, pack some love. Love is the currency of life, and as such, it is accepted everywhere around the world.

At the beginning of this book, you were asked to spend just fifteen minutes a day with God and to make it a habit. Good healthy habits will serve you well throughout life. Consider adding some more. Routines come in handy, especially spiritual ones. They keep you on course when life gets difficult.

Saint John of the Cross once wrote, "My spirit has become dry because it forgets to feed on you." He knew that we all need spiritual nourishment every day. May you continue to feast upon the goodness of God, and may you taste of his love and forgiveness.

P.S.—Congratulations on completing this spiritual trek!

PRAYER

Dear God, thank you for walking with me all the days of my life. Continue to stay by my side. Help me spend time with you each day. There is so much more that I need to know. You have so much more to teach me. Open my eyes and my ears. Show me where you want me to be. Amen.

FOCUS FOR THE DAY

Today I will celebrate the six-week anniversary of my closer walk with God.

Reflect on what you want to do now that you have completed your reading in this book. Think about what you have learned. Consider how you have changed.

How Are Things Going?
Week Six

For instructions on using the chart below, see page 31.

		Sun	Mon	Tues	Wed	Thurs	Fri	Sat
Daily Devotion	Date							
	Scripture							
	Devotion							
	Prayer							
	Focus for the Day							
	Reflection Time							
Daily Prayers	Morning							
	Meals							
	Bedtime							
	Other							